Beyond BIM

Beyond BIM explores the vast and under-explored design potential undertaken by information modeling. Through a series of investigations grounded in the analysis of built work, interviews with leading practitioners, and speculative projects, the author catalogs the practical advantages and theoretical implications of exploiting BIM as a primary tool for design innovation. Organized by information type, such as geographic data, local code, or material characteristics, each chapter suggests a realm of knowledge that can be harvested and imported into BIM to give meaningful specificity to architectural form and space. While highly sustainable, the work documented and envisioned in this book moves well beyond "normalization," to reveal inventive takes on contemporary practice.

Beyond BIM serves as a primary resource for professional architects from practice, researchers and designers engaged in information-related spatial design processes, as well as students and faculties of architecture schools in search of BIM design inspiration. Likewise, those highly attuned to computation and unconventional ways of creating form and space, particularly built outcomes that utilize BIM, will find this book meaningful and essential.

Danelle Briscoe is an Assistant Professor at the University of Texas at Austin School of Architecture. She received a Master of Architecture degree from Yale University (2002) and Bachelor of Architecture from the University of Texas at Austin with Honors (1995). Her practice experience includes project designer for Frank Gehry Partners, LLP and Marmol+ Radziner LLP. In addition to numerous conference publications, she has more notably published a chapter in *BIM in Academia* (Yale School of Architecture 2011) and is also the key researcher using BIM for the Austin Green Wall Initiative.

Beyond BIM
Architecture Information Modeling

Danelle Briscoe

LONDON AND NEW YORK

First published 2016
by Routledge
2 Park Square, Milton Park, Abingdon, Oxon OX14 4RN

and by Routledge
711 Third Avenue, New York, NY 10017

Routledge is an imprint of the Taylor & Francis Group, an informa business

© 2016 Danelle Briscoe

The right of Danelle Briscoe to be identified as author of this work has been asserted by her in accordance with sections 77 and 78 of the Copyright, Designs and Patents Act 1988.

All rights reserved. No part of this book may be reprinted or reproduced or utilized in any form or by any electronic, mechanical, or other means, now known or hereafter invented, including photocopying and recording, or in any information storage or retrieval system, without permission in writing from the publishers.

Trademark notice: Product or corporate names may be trademarks or registered trademarks, and are used only for identification and explanation without intent to infringe.

British Library Cataloguing-in-Publication Data
A catalogue record for this book is available from the British Library

Library of Congress Cataloging-in-Publication Data
Briscoe, Danelle, author, interviewer.
Beyond BIM : architecture information modeling / Danelle Briscoe.
pages cm
Includes bibliographical references and index.
1. Building information modeling. 2. Architects--Interviews. 3. Marble, Scott, 1960- I. Title. II. Title: Beyond building information modeling.
TH438.13.B74 2015
720.285–dc23
2015004909

ISBN: 978-1-138-78248-8 (hbk)
ISBN: 978-1-138-78249-5 (pbk)
ISBN: 978-1-315-76899-1 (ebk)

Typeset in Minion Pro by
Servis Filmsetting Ltd, Cheshire, Stockport

Printed and bound in the United States of America by Sheridan Books, Inc. (a Sheridan Group Company).

To Whit, Noel and Julian

Contents

Foreword by Peggy Deamer viii
Acknowledgments x
Author's note xii
Abbreviations xiii

1 Introduction 1

   Chapter / Interview:
2 Cultural data / Scott Marble 15
3 Point taken / Elena Manferdini 41
4 Environmental fact or fiction / Jeanne Gang 67
5 Material practice / Julie Eizenberg 97
6 Geomimicry / Greg Lynn 127
7 BIM landscape / Diana Balmori 157
8 Data central / Marc Fornes 185
9 bigBIM / Christopher Sharples and John Cerone 211

10 Conclusion 237

Index 244

Foreword

I CAN think of many advantages of this book: it does away with the misperception that BIM is about production, not design; that BIM leads to projects that are organizationally brilliant but aesthetically dull; that information, which BIM is so good at providing, hinders intuition and inspiration; that the value of parametrics in architecture is primarily formal; that only slide-ruler-type men participate in BIM; that BIM is just the next representational tool after AutoCad. All of these myths Danelle Briscoe does away with, with clarity, eloquence, and evidence. I need not elaborate them here. What may not be as obvious, however, is Briscoe's demonstration that architectural theory and practice can no longer be separated, brought together by a new definition of "research."

Briscoe and I first connected when teaching in Auckland, NZ, at a conference asking "What is research in architecture?" Since university funding in the Antipodes is directly linked to departmental research output, this was an urgent question for architecture, a discipline that in New Zealand doesn't indulge in cultural theory (and thus conform to the humanities' model of intellectual research) or experimental practices yielding "discoveries" (and thus conform to a scientific model of research). I remember Briscoe's presentation: she showed student design work from a second-year studio that used Revit to explore the formal opportunities of a simple program in an Auckland urban site. There was not much understanding of what she was claiming, but her (and her students') clear pleasure in design gave a hint that she was approaching this software in a radically different way than the norm. In hindsight, it was the beginning of not just Briscoe's sustained (and not common enough) belief in the creative nature of BIM, but research into the relationship between information and practice, knowledge and production, thought and artifact.

My claim that this book bridges theory and practice by demonstrating the breadth of BIM-generated intellectual research might seem self-evident. After all, if we take "theory" to mean, as is common today, a body of knowledge examining "the digital revolution," the distance between theory and practice is very small (and BIM's facilitation of this clear). But if we understand architectural theory in the more traditional sense – exploring the latent phenomena that shape architecture as a human (or post-human) condition – the claim is different. This broader sense of theory has had, in general, two different strains: one exploring the conditions that shape architectural design: proportions, typology, precedent, materials, communities, ecology, etc.; the other linking discourses outside of architecture proper – philosophy, cultural studies, gender studies, biopolitics, capitalism, etc. – to architectural disciplinarity. The contents of this book address both of these versions of theory. Questions ranging from the cultural identity of architects in a crowd-sourcing environment to the reading of objects that are animated, intelligent, and "live twice," virtually and physically are raised; the thought that design is nothing more than managing a virtual shop is entertained; and formal anxiety brought by the dialectic between the object and the surfaces that compose it or between mimicry, geometry, and imagination are explored. This is all unearthed by the vast array of unconventional practices covered by Briscoe in this book, practices that can only be called – whether profit-driven or not – "research."

This is not to say that the theoretical questions raised by BIM and Briscoe are answered. Observations made here about data and its ability to shape a humanist, quotidian approach to architecture, for example, need to be placed against more skeptical positions identifying data's (not always well) hidden invasion of privacy and of its proprietary organizers who benefit from data's collection and storage. Optimistic views about new forms of work – shared, open sourced, creative, and flexible – need to be read in the context of its "other": a never ending and frequently outsourced labor. But the pleasure of this book is Briscoe's identification of the larger issues at stake in a method of design that goes well beyond procurement and representational efficiency.

The fact that a relatively new technology – BIM – brings these theoretical issues with it is its most interesting feature. It disrupts every given convention about the author, the object, and the audience that the discipline has held dear. As Briscoe makes evident, if we don't embrace this aspect of BIM, we are either misguided or cowards.

Peggy Deamer
January, 2015

Acknowledgments

This book is greatly indebted on many counts to the University of Texas Office of the President for Research. I have been awarded several funding opportunities that have helped stimulate my scholarly initiatives toward this Building Information Modeling (or BIM) research, as well as assistance in the production of this publication. The 2009–2010 Research Grant Award, 2011 Big XII Faculty Fellowship Award, 2012 Tenure-Track Summer Research Assignment Award, 2013–2014 Subvention Grant Award and most recently the 2013–2014 Special Research Grant have all contributed and impacted this outcome. Internal funding from the University of Texas, School of Architecture Research Seed Award in 2012 also helped initiate a new ecological direction with BIM.

It is also important to acknowledge my history with this topic, and those that affected my early teaching career and building research. Tony Van Raat, Head of the School of Architecture at Unitec New Zealand, put trust in me to initiate digital thinking within that school, and was extremely supportive throughout my time there (2005–2009) as a Tenured Lecturer. Other faculty at Unitec SCALA, such as Jeanette Budgett, David Rhodes, Jeremy Treadwell, Padma Naidu, Glennis Grieve, Ainsley O'Connell and John Pusateri, in one way or another improved my thinking and motivated this investigation in its very early stages. Invitations to serve as Visiting Professor or Critic from other institutions, such as the Architectural Association in London, and the University of Auckland, School of Architecture, have allowed me to further test and provoke the topic of information modeling and push the work in alternative directions. I treasure the students' input and outcomes from the early "Beauty + the BIM" courses I taught in all these architectural institutions, which gave context to the work and helped push my thinking for the agenda of this book.

It is very necessary to thank Autodesk for their unending support in my research and teaching endeavors. Nancy Clark Brown kept me abreast for several years of their software developments, while Zach

Kron's research and development with Autodesk Revit, Vasari and now Dynamo continues to this day to be an inspiration for the future of my work with BIM.

Francesca Ford, Commissioning Editor for Architecture at Routledge, approached me in 2009 about writing a book and has since been supporting and believing in my project. Routledge Editorial Assistant Trudy Varcianna deserves countless thanks for the many questions she answered on behalf of this production, as well as Jennifer Birtill. The help of editorial advisors – Nancy Eklund, Stacy Patton, Joyce Rosner and Sam Dodd – clarified the content of this book in ways that I never could have achieved on my own. Laura Wagner was and is a rock-star graphic assistant, designer and moral supporter in the very early submissions of this proposal.

Peggy Deamer was an influential instructor in my graduate studies at Yale, but has more so in recent years become a mentor to my academic career. She continually supports all my requests for letters of recommendations and had much to do with my inclusion in the Yale BIM Symposium of 2010. I am very honored that she has agreed to write the foreword for this book.

In the past year, I have sacrificed much time away from my young family in order to write and stay focused on this topic and project. It is mostly to you, Whit, that I owe the production of this book and I am also eternally grateful for your love and support.

With my deepest gratitude, I thank you all.

Author's note

I come from a generation of designers that remembers the card catalog and saw the inception of computers in the design studio. At the tail end of my undergraduate studies in 1995, architectural practice was struggling with the birth of CAD – hatch patterns were crashing the files, sheets were abundant with discrepancies, and drawing count proliferation. Later in graduate school (Y2K), fabrication technologies, such as laser-cutters and CNC tools, were just starting to be put in place. Frank Gehry, my final studio professor at Yale, offered me a job just after my last review. Working for Frank, I saw the real benefits of using (what was then) the first actual application of BIM (i.e., CATIA). When I first started teaching the dos and don'ts of Revit to young Kiwis in 2005, I thought: "Right on. . . . This is CATIA for the rest of us."

In the 10+ years since those experiences, much has changed. Humans have undeniably become vehicles for data. From fuel bands to cell phone usage, data are being generated and behavior tracked in the (ostensible) service of a better understanding of our lives and the planet we live on. And that information is becoming increasingly a part of what energizes our design work. Speculating where BIM will go, beyond its current predominant provision to buildings and their elements, my sense is that the future will drive all this data and harvest it in new ways that we have yet to fully appreciate. This book introduces a unique perspective on the use of BIM in contemporary architectural practice, but also advocates the BIM model as an active, essential, and currently under-explored agent in the advancement of innovative design. With the rapid rate of technological change, there is a large chance that some specifics of this book will appear outdated by the time of publication, so if nothing more, *Beyond BIM: Architecture Information Modeling* holds a place for posterity to reflect on the technological transformation that is upon us.

Abbreviations

API	Application Programming Interface
BDS	Building Description System
BIM	Building Information Modeling
CAD	Computer Aided Design
CCTV	Closed-Circuit Television
CDR	Computational Design and Research (team)
CIM	City Information Modeling
CLT	Cross Laminated Timber
CNC	Computer Numerically Controlled
CSV	Comma-Separated Variables, List-Directed Input
CTL	Continuous Tangential Line
DCIM	Data Center Infrastructure Management System
DEM	Digital Elevation Model
FCD	Future Construction Demonstrator
FIM	Fabrication Information Modeling
FM	Facilities Maintenance
GIS	Geographic Information System
GPS	Global Positioning System
HCCB	High Capacity Color Barcode
IFC	Industry Foundation Class
IPD	Integrated Project Delivery
KML	Keyhole Markup Language
LCA	Life Cycle Assessment
LIM	Landscape Information Modeling
NURB	Non-Uniform Rationally Based
RSS	Rich Site Summary
TIN	Triangulated Irregular Network
TMI	Too Much Information
VDC	Virtual Design And Construction

1
Introduction

More so than ever before, humans access and exchange information effortlessly. In even the most remote reaches of the planet, any fact, figure, or contact number can be requested, and the information is returned instantaneously. And so every minute of every day, human interactions generate 204 million emails, 100,000 tweets, and 640 trillion bytes of data.[1] The prediction of an information-based virtual reality – the forward-thinking notion of cyberspace discussed only 25 years ago – is no longer a high-tech fantasy, but a practical reality.[2] As such, the broad extent and rapid rate of data transfer has redefined global culture, and transformed the tools and methods of architectural design.

At the core of this shift in architecture is the wide-scale adoption of Building Information Modeling (BIM) – the process by which a digital representation of a building's physical and functional characteristics is created, maintained, and shared as a knowledge resource. Since the early 2000s, BIM has become a necessary part of new building construction. But as architects and other design professionals have grown familiar with the modeling process, concerns have arisen. BIM is an effective tool to support the practical aspects of construction – like standard documentation, project management, and sustainability – but this focus has led critics to fear that BIM is driving the "normalization" of architecture, suppressing design innovation, and sacrificing formal and spatial expression for procedural clarity and building efficiency.

In the contemporary information-space, practitioners have the capacity to explore and incorporate large quantities of data in their work. Armed with new technological advances, the discipline of architecture is working to understand the broader implications for design and how the outcome of this shift from traditional industry to an ever-changing, information-based architecture sufficiently describes, guides, and executes the dynamics of a modern, complex society.

Beyond BIM explores the vast design potential of BIM. Through a series of investigations grounded in the analysis of built work, interviews with leading practitioners, and speculative academic projects, this

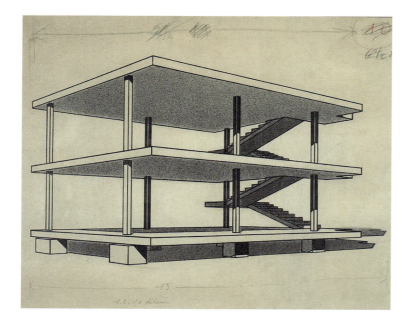

Le Corbusier Maison, Domino (1914 Plan FLC 19209A © F.L.C./ADAGP, Paris/Artists Rights Society (ARS), New York, 2014)

book catalogs the practical advantages and theoretical implications of exploiting BIM as a necessary tool for design innovation. Organized by information type, workflows, and material characteristics, each chapter defines a realm of knowledge that could be harvested for BIM, giving meaningful specificity to architectural form, space, and field. The work documented and envisioned in this book moves well beyond "normalization" to reveal inventive takes on contemporary practice.

Building

When considering the meanings behind the BIM acronym, "building" sets up a predicament from the perspective of design. As much as the discipline is in need of a construction protagonist – one that can strengthen the alleged declining relationship between architect and contractor and the general building organization – no one wants to produce just a *building*. The term has become a pejorative, associated with the most meaningless ways to cover space, like cheap commercial buildings and sheds. In contrast, architects want to design masterly space and form – in other words, architecture.[3] The discipline admires the act, not the artifact, of building. In this context, whereby orthogonal assumptions put forth nothing more than a box, "building" falls prey to the regularity of the datum and grid structure that is at the heart of the BIM construction plane. The nefarious nature of BIM lies in this conflict between building and designing.

Le Corbusier's 1914 *Maison Dom-ino* proposal exemplifies an orthogonal system of procedural clarity and building efficiency, and in many ways it represents the criticism of BIM. When taken literally (as it often is), its reinforced concrete frame is deployed in support of "building" instead of liberating the wall, as was originally intended by the system. Architecture critic Jeffrey Kipnis suggests a frequent mishandling of this framework, datum, and grid lines of inquiry in the potential design phase.[4] By allowing the grid and datum to limit visionary thinking – or at the very least, some aspects of innovation – the corresponding ground plane could generate a standard datum of architecture. Confidence in the coordinate system and framework supplied by BIM makes crucial differences plausible to the planar condition and to the breakdown of building as a system of parts – column, beam, footing – related to the whole.

Information

Historically, critical information for representing and creating architecture incorporated extensive amounts of human engineering data – compiled and disseminated in physical references and tools, such as *Architectural Graphic Standards*, Ernst Neufert's *Architects' Data* diagrams, and Henry Dreyfuss's *Human Scale–Body Measurement* cards. The *Human Scale* hand cards are literally human scale, pictorial selectors equipped with rotary dials of information. Each card, which contains three selectors (two sides each) encompassing basic anthropometric guidelines for human proportions, offers specific ergonomic dimensions for age and gender demographics useful to a project at hand. The numerical values given in these documents represented at the time the most up-to-date research from anthropologists, psychologists, scientists, human engineers, and medical experts and held an authority in the design studio. The intention was to expand the notion of "form follows function" and to encompass the idea that human data has influence: "form follows function follows data." For example, human physical measurements may dictate the design of a particular spatial function related to ergonomic activity, like sitting at a desk.

By offering 20,000 bits of information, the *Human Scale* pictorial cards appeared to be full of possibility as "design tools." These novel devices, with their toy-like, unique ability to determine values for data accessibility, inspired information-based design through gadgetry. Although they now serve as a precursor to the "parametric slider" (so commonly used in contemporary parametric design), the selectors offered up numerical values that ultimately relayed and promoted normative conditions. But what of the dynamic eccentricities of human movement, or bodies with atypical proportions? Rather than generating for difference, these historical data sets tended to frame critical dimensions as fixed standards, or as Nicholas Negroponte put it, "a demographic unit of one."[5]

The emerging information paradigm in architecture supports design mediated by the ability of a designer to capture and employ information freely with the potential for innovation. The success that informational modeling and data visualization has been met with in science and other disciplines suggests that the potential advantages of incorporating infinite amounts of data available today into the design process far outweigh the dangers.[6] Rather than viewing BIM as a liability, architects should re-conceive the platform as a tool for pushing their own, unique conceptual agendas, or those generating for difference. BIM has the potential to enhance the design process in ways that will transform the resulting architecture.

This position of information-driven design suggests a criticality of intuition in the conceptualization of architecture. The access to granular information would have at one time seemed unimportant, or difficult (if not impossible) to find or incorporate. And yet, current data-capture and input technology, with its hyper-sensitivity to what is minute or obscure, implies design opinion as it pointedly changes the way facts are generated, collected, and implemented in an architectural project. As seen in the work of MAP Architects during their *Svalbard Architectural Expedition*, contemporary practitioners are increasingly testing innovative design methods by creating data-recording devices to tailor the information to conditional specificity. Producing unique data sets, not just harvesting incomplete or generalized ones, gets to the heart of information's usefulness to design. In the case of MAP Architects, one of the "design instruments" created a spectrometer by de-constructing a webcam. This instrument was intended to register "spectral information" responsible for the color and altitude of the aurora borealis. This data, paired with video and photographic recordings of the aurora, furthered the design team's understanding of the processes that create the spectacle – processes that might now be co-opted for innovative architectural agendas.

Human Scale 1/2/3: Body Measurements (image courtesy of Niels Diffrient, Alvin R. Tilley, and Joan Bardagjy, MIT Press; Bk&Acces edition, 1974) Photo credit Whit Preston

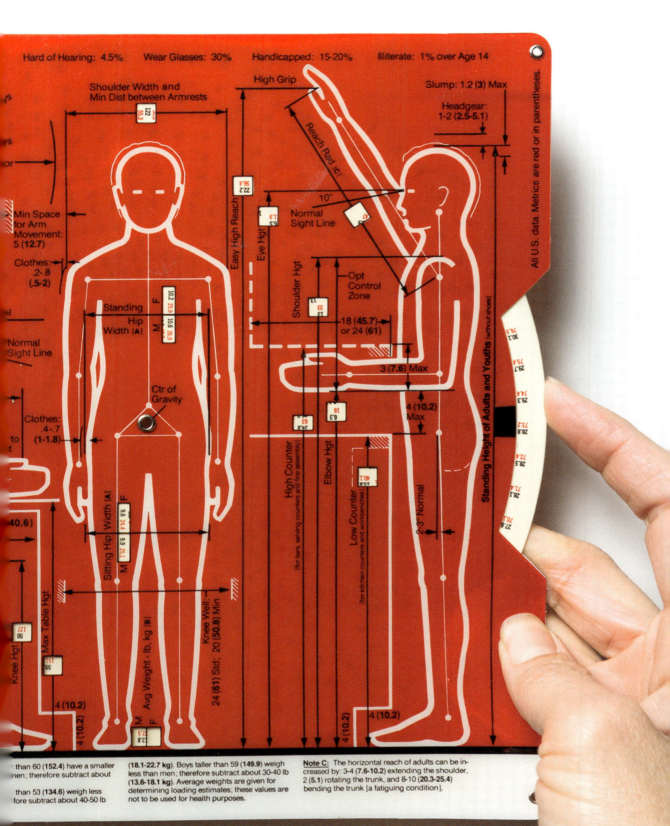

Svalbard Architectural Expedition (image provided by MAP Architects, 2013)

Modeling

Much of the basis for form creation in the BIM environment can be mapped to the earliest patriarchal software developments. In the 1970s, computer-aided design (CAD) rendered design to drafted intentions of vectors of lines, points, curves, and planes. This platform, which emerged to address hand-drawing inefficiency and management discrepancy issues, escorted basic, orthogonal geometry into architecture. The process led to more rapid replication of partial drawings and a new by-product of layer management: drawings were graphically clear and offered ease of reproduction. Information, however, became more fragmented, and conflicts between documents increased. In this scenario where CAD vectors represented no intrinsic information (other than a definitive position and directionality on the x and y axes of the work plane), their input (like hand drafting), relied primarily on intuitive placement. As CAD systems were most powerful in standardized, modular, symmetrical designs, many designers and architects remained skeptical of CAD as a design tool, fearing these limited productivity features would have too strong an influence on their work. Similar fears have surrounded the emergence of BIM as another acronymic design tool.

Although a shift to the use of BIM is viewed as a fairly new way of discerning and producing architecture, Chuck Eastman described a

OPPOSITE

Images from the 1975 article "The Use of Computers Instead of Drawings in Building Design" (image courtesy of Chuck Eastman)

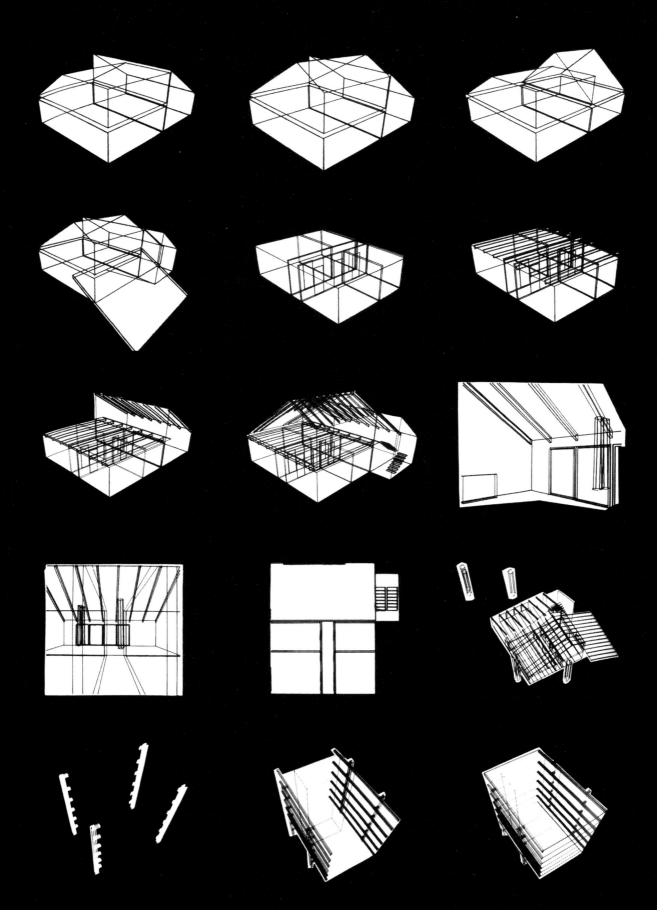

similar building information model 40 years ago. In his article "The Use of Computers Instead of Drawings in Building Design,"[7] what he then called a building description system (BDS) offered a virtual multi-view, architectural modeling system as an enabler of arrangements and three-dimensional building elements. Eastman's BDS focused on the design scale of a single building component. Such elements display the tectonic generation and iteration within a building design, providing a complete and coherent computer-based model of three-dimensional objects and their spatial arrangement. Today, there is still a reference to this Cartesian coordinate system, but it is viewed as a framework for building organization that promotes the play of difference rather than its literal translation. As a result of this early research, Eastman is the single person most referenced in the origins of BIM.[8]

BIM is also linked to the legacy of its software precursors, sharing their inherited benefits and possible drawbacks. From early on, Frank Gehry and subsequently Greg Lynn, disregarded the orthogonal ordinates of the industry's predominant CAD software for both physical and digital model-based approaches.[9] Traditionally, architects tended to produce a variety of preliminary drawings and studies that they then compressed into a rarefied or lean representational package. The industry grew up assigning control and responsibility based on these documents. This legacy prompted Gehry and Lynn (and those who followed) to look to alternative technological capabilities of object modeling from other disciplines, as opposed to building software. Gehry adopted a methodology from the aerospace sciences, intended for managing very large data sets of geometric information, and applied it to buildings. Lynn looked to the flexibility of animation software to provide creative solutions to architectural design problems and workflows. Lynn's competition entry for the *Port Authority Triple Bridge Gateway* was the first architectural project to ever use animation software for form generation. Lynn also focused more on the "forces" representing traffic (pedestrian flow with velocity and their changing paths) – research is now similarly being developed by BuroHappold's SmartMoves team as advanced BIM technique. These early workflows combined the power of object modeling with the compulsion for visualization, and subsequently established a new respect for shared knowledge between collaborators and consultants. The master-model approach established the idea of a cross-disciplinary, schematic design exchange, as seen in BIM. This design thinking pursues and trusts the information and knowledge

Port Authority Triple Bridge Gateway (image courtesy of Greg Lynn FORM)

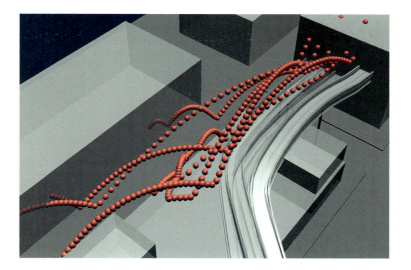

of others, then activates it in the modeling process for the needs of architectural specificity.

To model in BIM, a hierarchical framework establishes opportunities for regularity where irregularity and difference can co-exist. This virtual construct can build up geometry, sequentially starting with planar elements that act like a physical jig and allow for more control of complexity. Architects can structure the formal, data-based design problem this way: identifying principal geometric drivers or reference planes, and modeling those with geometric primitives like lines, points, and planes. Analogous to how one models in BIM, the physical means of 'constructing' architecture requires the use of a coordinate system made from basic construction planes. These intersecting, right-angled surfaces are necessary to rationalize the physical geometry demonstrating formal complexity and spatial eccentricity. The *Organic Design in Home Furnishings: Relaxation Chair Competition* entry by Charles and Ray Eames demonstrates an early example of this reliance on a modern system. For the Eameses, a jig controlled the spatial location and directionality of other desired inputs for the body, and physical mockups of the design could increase in scale.

A default BIM database operates from a surplus of detailed building parts and assemblies. This organization imposes a product-based structure onto a hierarchical arrangement of the world. A BIM "smart" virtual object resembles the actual physical product in every detail, both in terms of its three-dimensional graphic representation and

Eames Organic Design in Home Furnishings: *Relaxation Chair*, 1941. (Copyright Cranbrook Archives, Richard G. Askew, photographer, 5652–3)

in terms of its embedded product data and properties. This information is utilized in scheduling the eventual construction of the building.

BIM components derive from a number of conditions: placeholders, originators, or borrowers. Placeholders form default embedded project content, such as walls, doors, windows, furniture, and so on. Typically, these items are standard to a generic building and represent those real items that can be delivered and installed on site. This would assume that a BIM library is a robust vessel to pluck from or provide a wealth of quasi, self-organizing entities. Skeptics use this placeholder condition to criticize the normalization of architecture resulting from BIM, as if selectivity can replace creativity. The process of originating unique instances of geometry and analyzing or otherwise using the information within a model platform unfolds through the control of parameters. In a neutral conceptual massing component, parametric design values allow a designer to create an adaptable situation of more complex relationships. Alternatively, a borrowed component can be downloaded directly from a manufacturer or external designer. This is a provision of manufacturers' products, some standard

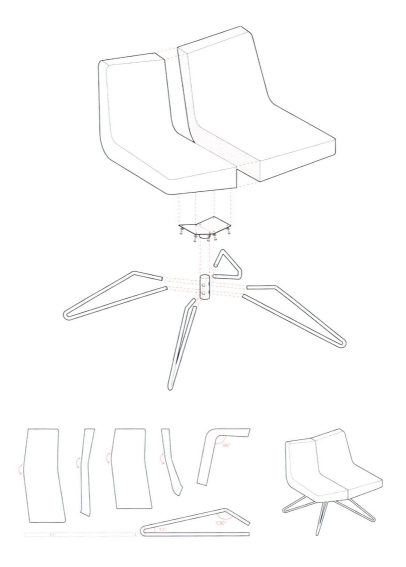

Big Hug Chair (model courtesy of BIMOBject.com/image extraction by Zach Walters)

and some of high design. If the BIM component inserts expediently into a project, it raises the question, again, of who controls or designs the information model and how long that control lasts. Companies such as *BIMObject* are replacing the more conventional *McGraw Hill Sweet's Catalogue* with provisions of cloud-based, fully modeled BIM entities, ready to download (either as open-source or for a nominal fee) into a project. The design is uploaded as a highly detailed and informed system that is then hosted by other designers in a definitive BIM environment. This exchange suggests a culture of collaboration, so to speak, in borrowing information from the workflows, opinions, and values of others.

Criticism of BIM has largely emanated from the forefronts of the computation, technology, and fabrication side of architectural practice and education. Vocal opponents, like Andrew Kudless, point out its steep learning curve, tendencies toward a belabored workflow and generally normative production. According to Kudless, "the database platform assumes too many conventional ways of thinking about the design process, especially with fundamental elements or features like a wall."[10] Advocates and early adopters of BIM counter this criticism by arguing for the value gained by information early on in the design process, which can be turned into knowledge sooner rather than later.

BIM interfaces, which have the power to process large amounts of data, face the reputation of being "information excessive" for most architects. As a result, BIM software is more likely to be adopted by larger firms that tend toward production of the corporate norm. While owning and mastering the use of this software might currently be viewed as prohibitive, it is important to consider that, as a representational system, BIM neither enforces nor endorses one particular or singular piece of software. Rather, it can accommodate and be supported by a range of design and construction platforms and more importantly serve as a communication system between whichever software each discipline feels works best for them. The following chapters survey the multitude of data origins, file types, platforms, and workflows that produce the amalgamation of a single, collaborative data-based design source.[11] BIM, and its capabilities for building, information processing, and modeling, has arrived as a long-needed disruption to traditional methods of representation, collaboration, and implementation of architecture. Advances in modeling (and its future speculation) provide greater control of quantification, characteristics, and behavior of construction information – bringing ever closer the artifice of virtual completeness and defining relationships between modeled components of data and the world of architecture.

Notes
1. Rick Burgess, "One Minute on the Internet," *Techspot.com*, March 20, 2013, www.techspot.com/news/52011-one-minute-on-the-internet-640tb-data-transferred-100k-tweets-204-million-e-mails-sent.html.
2. Michael Benedikt, *Cyberspace: First Steps* (Cambridge, MA: MIT Press, 1992).

3   Julie Lovine, "Art/Architecture: Building a Bad Reputation," *New York Times* (August 8, 2004).
4   Jeffrey Kipnis, "Discrimination" (presentation, Harvard Graduate School of Design, Cambridge, MA, October 18, 2006).
5   Negroponte, Nicolas. *Being Digital* (New York, NY: Vintage; 1st edition, 1996).
6   Manuel Lima, *Visual Complexity: Mapping Patterns of Information* (New York, NY: Princeton Architectural Press, 2013).
7   Chuck Eastman, "The Use of Computers Instead of Drawings in Building Design," *AIA Journal* 63, no. 3 (March 1975): 46–50.
8   Robert Aish, "Building Modeling: The Key to Integrated Construction CAD," in *Proceedings of the Fifth International Symposium on the Use of Computers for Environmental Engineering Related to Buildings*, D. Arnold, ed. (London: CIBSE, 1986). For more on this position, see "History of Building Information Modeling," http://codebim.com/resources/history-of-building-information-modeling.
9   For more on Frank Gehry and Greg Lynn, see Mildred Friedman, *Gehry Talks: Architecture + Process* (New York, NY: Universe Publishing, 2002); and Greg Lynn and Mark Rappolt, *Greg Lynn Form* (New York, NY: Rizzoli, 2008).
10 Andrew Kudless, interview with the author, February 22, 2013.
11 ArchiCAD, Digital Project, Bentley Generative Components, Autodesk Revit, and Nemetschek Vectorworks are all platforms that advertise as BIM capable.

2

Cultural data

Not so long ago, "Data" was best known as the fully functional, futuristic android who served as the second officer aboard the starship Enterprise. As an extension of Isaac Asimov's invention of the "positronic brain" and the general idea of robotics, this fictional character demonstrated impressive computational abilities, collecting and processing his namesake – data – from the far reaches of the physical universe. Sentient and self-aware, he possessed a form of consciousness, if not human, then recognizable to humans.

Today, data is you, everyone you know, and no longer a fiction. Exponential in size, it is the sum total of what we know: all the bits of information that are generated – quantitative and qualitative, distant and proximate, virtual and real – which are then collected, digitized, and made available for analysis by global institutions like Google. The logistics of your everyday life – your comings and goings, social and buying habits, opinions and emotions – have become raw material for a wide range of professionals, from film producers to politicians, who use it to embed cultural resonance in their product or content.[1] Architecture, now charged with a data-based design environment, can be equally responsive to the culture of its constituency. This chapter brings together projects that turn cultural data into an active agent for social engagement, cultural continuity, and reflection.

To some, the use of cultural data in the design of buildings may be seen as a reaction to a century of architecture based on ideals of objectivity. Modern architects of the International Style emerging in the 1920s sought solutions that transcended cultural associations or predilections. Prior styles representing national or regional uniqueness were eschewed in favor of an aesthetic grounded in the expression of function and materials. Within the current information paradigm, however, architecture can account for cultural and emotional factors by applying data to questions of function and materiality, albeit not through traditional means of representation or through stylistic adherence. Rather, through data-gathering and information-storing technologies,

Data from *Star Trek* (image courtesy of wallpaperstock.net)

cultural aspects (identified as relevant by an architect) are transforming modeled geometry, the BIM space of collaboration, and in effect the built environment.

Data gathered

Information passed down from one generation to the next happens vertically – grandmother to mother to daughter, etc. Cultural information, however, transmits between neighbors of the same generation or diffuses between social groups laterally, meaning cultural evolution can be extremely rapid, particularly when the transmission is digital.[2] Collecting this cultural behavior through either cell phone data, digital surveys, network monitoring, or Twitter feeds can lead to input in support of experimental operations of applied BIM. These data flows enable designers to explore vastly larger interest groups and alternative classes of information. This new skill extends design investigation: Is the purpose of a column to transfer structural load, appeal as an architectural element, or carry and embed cultural connotations?

Data-producing devices are as ubiquitous as they are varied, from personal laptops and cell phones to more specialized equipment such as biometric pedometer bands and watches. The growing interest in attaining personal information within contemporary society creates obvious fodder for design intentions, even if its arbitrary application runs the risk of suspicion and provokes concern about privacy and surveillance.[3] All of these individual and informal movements, behaviors, and transactions fill the gaps in a growing and participatory data set that exists outside the formal economy. Collective accounts of the life and culture of a city, such as MyBlockNYC.com, are becoming a more conscious demonstration of the sort of interactive mapping that captures and defines the minutia of culture. In this case individual users can upload videos embedded with geospatial data, creating an intimate, evolving, and complete portrait of an urban space. This individualized, cultural data set provides more explicit input and is foreseeably applicable as agency in a design scenario using BIM by the masses.

In consideration of an architecture that takes on the beat of personal opinion and minutia, Diller Scofidio + Renfro activated the notion of cultural data input with their vanguard *Blur Building* in 2002. Executed at a time well before the general acceptance of crowd sourcing

Blur Building emotional states potentially captured by the "braincoat" (images courtesy of Diller Scofidio + Renfro, copyright Beat Widner), coupled with new emoticons used for expressing behavioral states (image credit Danelle Briscoe)

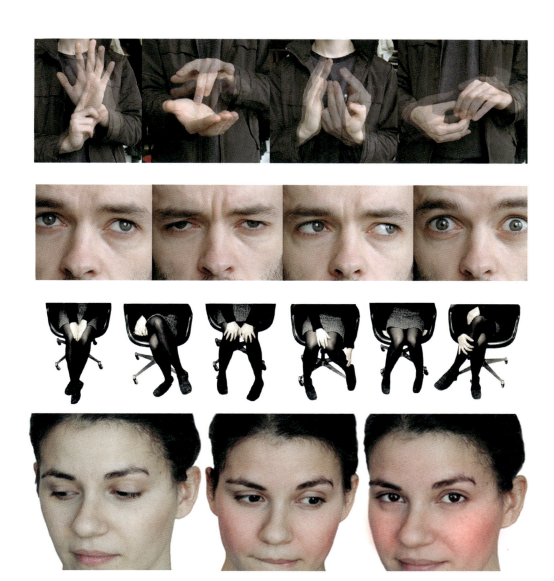

Check one:

☐ Sinner or Saint ☐

☐ Beauty or Beast ☐

☐ Puccini or Prince ☥ ☐

☐ Most or Least ☐

☐ Saunter or Mince ☐

☐ Fight or Faint ☐

☐ One love or Two ☐

☐ Old World or New ☐

☐ Back Door, ☐ Front Door, Do Not Enter ☐

☐ Left or ☐ Right or Center ☐

☐ Separate, Overlap ☐

☐ Satin or Burlap ☐

Blur Building "braincoat" questionnaire (images courtesy of Diller Scofidio + Renfro, copyright Beat Widmer)

or BIM was an industry standard, this pavilion used a decidedly low-tech binary questionnaire to attain values from its visitors. Answers were then incorporated into the aesthetic and experiential qualities of the formless space and event. As part of the Swiss National Expo, the temporary metal framework suspended above Lake Geneva in Yverdon-Les-Bains, Switzerland, was best known for its strategic inhabitable fog, created from a grid of 31,400 fog nozzles. The strength of the spray was digitally controlled and updated according to constantly changing climactic data conditions, such as temperature, humidity, wind speed, and direction. The fog mass was said to have expanded and produced long fog trails in high winds, rolled outward at cooler temperatures, and moved up or down depending on air temperatures.

The project no doubt broke many boundaries of a standard "building," but more importantly for this discussion, prompted the individual values and opinions of visitors to choreograph their own internal atmosphere. Walking down a long ramp, guests arrived at the center of the fog mass, where an outdoor platform and login station was modestly surrounded by the white noise and mist of pulsing water nozzles. Each visitor filled out a binary questionnaire, which produced an algorithm to be embedded as a light source into a unique raincoat, or "braincoat" as it was dubbed.[4] The visitor would wear this coat and move through the blurred space of the pavilion. The data-bearing coat then compared itself to that of others in the vicinity. Acting like a social radar, the coat literally blushed a warm pink light when it sensed a nearby compatible visitor, turned icy blue when approached by others of antipathy, and even vibrated in the presence of a completely symbiotic neighbor. The pulsating display created a secondary effect informed by an individualized belief system within the elusively defined boundary of the pavilion.

In the same way that a coat can become a social radar, urban conditions are ripe for opportunities to shift the impulses of the individual into a network of cultural expression. William Mitchell, in his seminal text *Me++: The Cyborg Self and the Networked City*, points out how the portability and miniaturization of communication technology in particular facilitates the exploration and interactions of humans in space.[5] The ability to control, for instance, the power that lights up an apartment, bus stop, or office through data exchange comes from the convergence of modern information technology, including geospatial recognition, connected network models for

20.08.13 10:00AM AUCKLAND

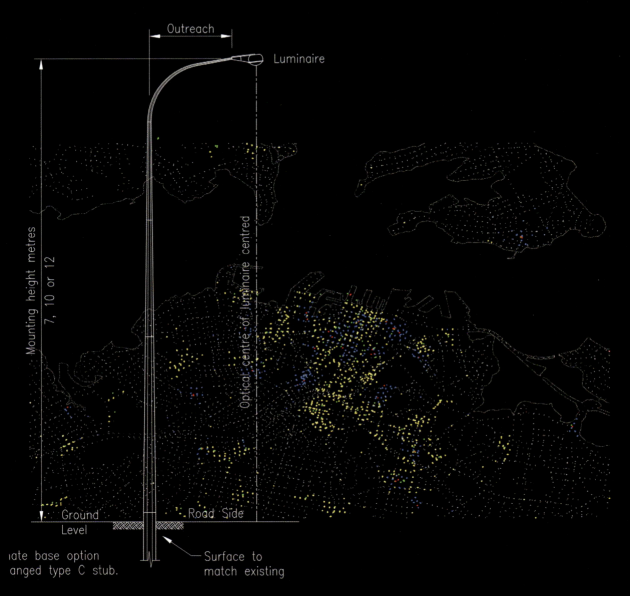

[0] "havsexy"
[1] "Trying a different route to work. :) (@ Britomart Transport Centre - @britomartnz w/ 3 others) http://t.co/5Ko1kqt369"
[2] "Thu Aug 15 08:56:48 NZST 2013"
[3] "Aug"
[4] "15"
[5] "08"
[6] "56"
[7] "48"
[8] "-36.844067"
[9] "174.76733"
[10] "-36.844402"
[11] "174.77368"
[12] "81.0"

Tweeting Streetlamp (image courtesy of Steven Lin, School of Architecture and Planning, the University of Auckland, Master of Architecture (Professional) Advanced Design 2 Studio, Visiting Professor Danelle Briscoe)

electric power, telecommunications, and other infrastructural, real-time data management systems, speculatively operating through BIM objects.[6]

In an attempt to focus this exploration, architecture has gained access to a generative method of linking external cultural data to a database. Through the implementation of programming applications in the design of urban space, Tweeters become co-contributors to the activation of space. In the *Tweeting Streetlamp* project, designed as part of an advanced studio at the University of Auckland's School of Architecture, large amounts of Twitter-user data stream to a common urban object, an everyday streetlamp. The inconspicuous and yet ever present source, Twitter, feeds into the real-time visualization of data to stimulate novel networks of urban identity and cultural emotion. The streetlamp can now be designed (or retrofitted) to react through lamp color to the emotional feed of the Twitter users. For example, the input of a smiley face/hash tag (☺/) emoticon displays as a color according to whatever symbol is used during any time of day or night in a given area of a city. This BIM element physically translates the data typed into Twitter from the individual's portable mobile device. In effect, points in space are given an identity, uniting and ultimately altering physical space as it is tied to its ephemeral nature, much like the data itself. In this way, the project evokes Mitchell's notion of urban communities developing around a necessary resource, such as a campfire or elemental hearth.[7] Here, the industrialized equivalent, the urban street light, takes its place as essential infrastructure for an around-the-clock presence in today's civilization.

In this case, the lighting construct is the BIM portal – an object model that distributes the parsed *Twitter* feeds freely, spontaneously, and automatically. Such a speculation would obviously require some mechanistic upgrade to the existing streetlights, but is not inconceivable in relation to what is possible with data translation. The recombination of data in the BIM streetlamp speaks to the lifecycle of the model and who controls the output (to be later discussed in another chapter). Does the culture of independent users tweeting emoticons in a vicinity drive the lighting network based on their spontaneous input? Such an expression of emotional occupancy highlights the current existence of a dynamic urban condition.

Once active, the Twitter occurrence could be played up as a performance of color and light, subside as an indiscernible effect (like the

Blur Building), or form a new system of communication that deals with the individual human condition at the urban scale. The design resource – data fragmentation in the form of geo-location tweets – is mobile and widely used. The ability to recombine expressions of emotions, or any other quantifiable topic, within a network is a democratic organization with limitless (other than the constraint of the Twitter word count) possibilities for application or usage.

To bring cultural expression to bear in practice, the design process becomes more conscious and adept at deploying these data sets from individual and group behaviors. Interactive devices are now borrowed from digital gaming to serve architecture with a new dexterity – one that eventually aims to visualize the cultural desires through interactivity of participants. Aedas, a leading global architecture and design practice, maintains this interest in human-centric design generation through their research of live contexts, either via "big data" simulation or virtual reality (VR) conditions. Their Computational Design and Research (CDR) team utilizes BIM, but not necessarily in the prosaic sense. Instead, CDR develops applications that emphasize idiosyncratic properties of space and human occupation in particular.[8] The *Future Construction Demonstrator* (FCD) is one such prototype developed for the Fraunhofer Institute of Germany, Europe's largest application-oriented research organization. Fraunhofer itself develops applications for people's needs, such as health, security, and communication. Logically, their own facility became a pilot project for the FCD application to relate employee participation and manufacturing constraints to the design of their own company space.

The FCD, according to Christian Derix, Director of the Aedas CDR:

> Represents a pedagogical model to reveal to all stakeholders how spatial planning decisions affect each other. The process resolves interdependencies of spaces without solving for optimal targets. In fact, the simulations for layout design and use allocation revealed new spaces where social functions could occur from a confluence of user gathering. This simulation prolongs the design process by highlighting missed opportunities. This is done by looking at the occupants' behavior rather than area efficiencies. So, our pursuit is for the "optimal affordance of use" rather than optimal cost of a building design. FCD has two algorithmic models built in that

Future Construction Demonstrator (image provided by Aedas Computational Design and Research)

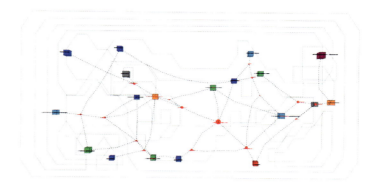

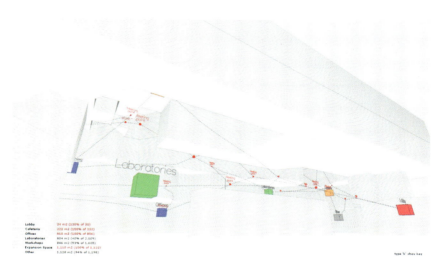

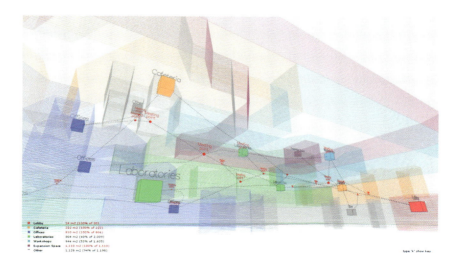

proposes new affordances from the data input, which is a) potential social spaces from circulation properties as a network of flows by area allocation; and b) circulation network from allocation of access points to functions. Both to do with interpreting access structures and movement behaviors. As opposed to the standard BIM packages, CDR develops the heuristics of a design methodology because that is where the 'intuitive knowledge' resides.[9]

The FCD model provides a perceptive link between the interpretation of the building program distribution, the building designer, and the encoded network algorithms. The building designer manipulates the occupants' movement networks interactively, while immersed in the VR set-up. A correlation between "design actions" and "user behaviors" is viscerally established by sharing the same representation and perceived dynamic in real time. More simply put, the actual behavior from employees becomes monitored VR data where impromptu meeting points occur and for how long. This information is exported to a database, like BIM, where another simulation or model of spaces resides. This means that the two area programs and circulation networks are linked and developing simultaneously, addressing both the concerns and the interdependence of the database and the user. Derix describes the potential of an "open framework" for a whole host of models to co-exist within BIM that allow for longer involvement and earlier start in the strategic design phase. Alternative models for the interior interrogate detailed design of surfaces or workplace arrangements, while models of public planning decision appraisal reveal post-planning visualization.

Cultural component

Historically, architectural design gathers community opinion through a process resembling a "town hall" meeting. This type of public outreach has been frequently criticized for finding the lowest common denominator, or becoming a veiled attempt to rationalize preconceived design strategies and navigate around any potential public resistance. In the case of *Superkilen Park*, a public urban square in the Nørrebro district of Copenhagen, Denmark, Bjarke Ingels Group (BIG) relied on public participation as the driving force of the design. With landscape architects Topotek 1 and the artist group Superflex, this collaborative

View of culturally loaded street lamps at *Superkilen Park*, Denmark (image courtesy of Bjarke Ingels Group)

team recognized the potential for a project to integrate user information and actually highlight cultural biases, rather than pushing an aesthetic exercise in Danish design. The site, a one-kilometer space along the tracks of a former rail yard, occupies the most ethnically diverse neighborhood in all of Denmark, where more than 60 nationalities coexist peacefully within its small footprint.

The park's diversity of urban features extends from around the globe: a Venice Beach with Thai Boxing, Chinese pole dancing, and even an Estonian swing.[10] Ideas and artifacts were collected and interpreted through a method of alternative crowdsourcing, intended to ensure the maximum freedom of expression. This process included data from public meetings, a website opinion collector and disseminator, local newspapers, and even a physical ideas mailbox mounted in the neighborhood. The BIG project architect, Nanna Gyldholm Møller, notes:

> We learned that people do not just show up, you have to go out and get them to have [the desired information] from all layers of diversity (cultural, social, age, etc.). It is very important to [control] the part of the project that the users are a part of or at least ask very specific questions. For example at one point the neighbors were helping out choosing the red colors on the red square, and of course we ended up having a brown square! It's important to be specific.[11]

In a process such as this, the architect must contend with the multiplicity of design authorship extending from constituents of cultural opinion. Insertion of this opinion and to what degree it unfolds still relies on the design skills of the architect, making a designer invulnerable to a role of mere coordinator of information.[12] The ability to amass a tabular wish-list of urban elements forms the basis of a new design collaboration: peer-to-peer design, literally implemented. By transforming public procedure into proactive proposition, a park such as *Superkilen* stands as a real sampling of the diversity resulting from data input and embedding culture into architectural objects.

Continued Cultural input at Superkilen Park, Denmark (image courtesy of Bjarke Ingels Group)

Conclusion

Open-source data generosity befits a new culture of digital generation through information modeling. A willingness to share data, design workflows, information, and knowledge places emphasis on the

quality assurance of the sources, a concern that elevates the ability and strategies of a designer. Design must also discern relevance and parse out an excessive amount of open-source conditions to ensure it creates necessary design information and, ultimately, that it improves or creates qualitative results versus simply proliferating quantitative architecture. Both quantitative and resulting qualitative knowledge hold the potential to provide information feedback that would inevitably benefit the design phase and the resultant built work in architecture.

The current generation of architecture students is well beyond the fascination with technological formalism and rejects such notions of a direct translation of data. Instead, their interest is in the performance of data, and for that performance to be much better than the given BIM platforms at large. Designing from a source of cultural input, which arrives and disappears within a second, poses a challenge – one that inevitably returns to the idea of data fluidity and accessibility, as simply demonstrated by the Blur Building's temporal event. The temporality of input and output raises new questions in the debate regarding permanence and, consequently, architecture. Can information prompt form-generation directly from its users/client data input as an order of understanding public opinion? How fixed should this be? Integrating culture into an architectural proposition, using objects such as chairs, streetlights, and playground objects derived from data input and output, encourages a broader public contribution to design, and supports not only specific belief systems acquired by information technology, but also simultaneously reinforces individuality and diversity itself.

The virtuosity of these projects lies in their ability to relate information to or from a particular group or cultures into the built environment, even if hypothetically. BIG's *Superkilen Park* supports cultural diversity; Diller Scofidio + Renfro's *Blur Building* supports individuality and interaction on a different temporal level and calibrates space in a fleeting way via human presence. The *Blur Building* and Twitter-fed streetlamps create events that are in effect indiscernible and at the same time distinctly spatial and experiential – or, in effect, architectural.

Notes
1. Lev Manovich, "Cultural Analytics: Visualizing Cultural Patterns in the Era of 'More Media,'" *DOMUS* (March 2009).
2. Michael Weinstock, *The Architecture of Emergence* (Chichester: Wiley, 2010).
3. An awareness of this situation was prompted by the 2013 Edward Snowden leak that made

clear the National Security Agency collection of location data from five billion cell phones every day.
4   Diller Scofidio + Renfro drafted the questionnaire in collaboration with writer Douglas Cooper.
5   William Mitchell, *Me++, the Cyborg Self and the Networked City* (Cambridge, MA: MIT Press, 2003).
6   Geoff Zeiss, "Convergence of Geospatial and Building Information Modeling (BIM) Accelerates," *Between the Poles* (May 28, 2013), http://geospatial.blogs.com/geospatial/2013/05/convergence-of-geospatial-and-building-information-modeling-bim-accelerates.html.
7   Gottfried Semper, *The Four Elements of Architecture and Other Writings*, trans. Harry Francis Mallgrave and Wolfgang Herrmann (Cambridge: Cambridge University Press, 1989), pp. 101–127.
8   The former Computational Design Research group at Aedas is now at WoodsBagot.
9   Christian Derix, email to the author, July 21, 2014.
10 For BIG, the hope was that most of the 120 different plants, lamps, and pieces of furniture would be bought online and shipped to Denmark from their various countries. Due to Danish regulations (mainly regarding playgrounds), but also the fact that many of the original objects had been tailor-made, it turned out that BIG had to create copies of more than half of the items selected.
11 Nanna Gyldholm Møller, email to the author, February 21, 2014.
12 Branko Kolaravic, "Information Master Builders," *Architecture in the Digital Age: Design and Manufacturing* (New York, NY: Spon press, 2003), p. 60.

Bibliography
Negroponte, Nicholas. *Being Digital*. New York, NY: Vintage Books, 1995.

[INTERVIEW]

Scott Marble
MARBLE FAIRBANKS

Standard BIM techniques have gained the reputation of being simply a directive toward documentation, and to some extent provoking a more restrained approach to architectural design. How has BIM enabled Marble Fairbanks' design process and output to rise above this predilection?

As you suggest, BIM has been closely associated with the single objective of better and more efficient project documentation, even when its origins promise something very different. If you think about a model in the broadest sense as information capture that extends beyond just the geometric relationships of a building, the possibilities of a true shift in methodology and workflow are much greater than what is happening right now. The rate at which new and relevant data are being generated is much faster than our ability to incorporate them into our working methods. The pace of change within our industry is painfully slow, which makes quick, disruptive shifts in design and construction less likely than in other industries. I think the current limitations of BIM largely have to do with the deeply entrenched cultural constraints of the AEC industry, which has a hard time thinking outside itself. Our practice attempts to look for atypical types of information that is relevant for a particular project or client and utilize it as a conceptual basis for design. In other words, we use information within a model to both inform and explore design options.

The logistics of everyday life – comings and goings, social and economic habits, opinions and emotions – have become raw data for a wide range of professionals, from film producers to politicians. These disciplines use these data to embed cultural resonance in their product or content. How can architecture, using current and future capabilities in the BIM environment (or what it

Main entrance Glen Oaks Library (image courtesy of Marble Fairbanks, photo credit Eduard Hueber)

could be), be equally responsive to the culture of its constituency?

Well, this is what is truly exciting about the potential of BIM – to transform rigid working processes into data-rich, highly responsive design workflows. Social data are just one example of a new type of information that could become part of a BIM, with its own dashboard output to be considered by the design team along with more typical outputs like cost, energy performance, material takeoffs, etc. It might take a series of bold startups by young designers and builders unaffected by the current state of affairs to develop workflows that cull and organize these new types of information into useful and valuable formats for design and construction. It is likely that this will happen outside the current industry version of BIM. For instance, the new start up Flux, a Google X project, was recently launched to provide environmental data about sites in a user-friendly interface, and an architect was on the team. Environmental data are just the low-hanging fruit; as social data become more valuable to architectural design, there will be tremendous opportunities to transform how we design.

I think there's an opportunity to not only make a project more efficient through data, but to be more explicit and expedient with what a culture wants or needs.

Currently, the most valued data used to describe the attributes of a building revolve around cost, size, location, and other factors that are easy to quantify. Ideally, there would be greater and faster progress in collecting and synthesizing cultural data into useful formats for architects to utilize as design inputs. To expand our understanding of cultural dimensions through data gets messier yet potentially more interesting because it is more qualitative. There isn't an obvious single design solution that follows the rules of efficiency, but rather many solutions that require interpretation and judgment. In this case, data are informing design decisions but not explicitly driving them. However, if we are determining what a culture wants or needs through data and incorporating that data into a design workflow, the choices of which sources to use becomes an important design decision – the creative side to design expands to where early upstream decisions have greater downstream implications.

Window detail Glen Oaks Library (image courtesy of Marble Fairbanks, photo credit Eduard Hueber)

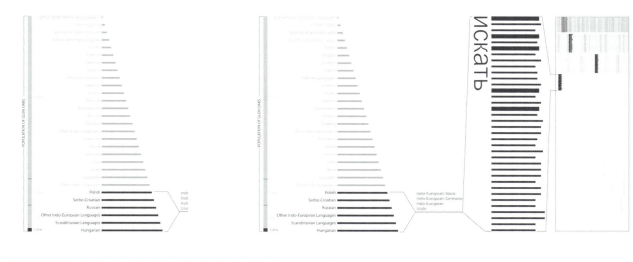

Your Glen Oaks Branch Library project in Queens, NY brings together cultural data as an active agent for social engagement, cultural continuity, and reflection. The graphic pattern on the north and west elevation explicitly demonstrates the ethnic diversity of its community while doubling as a screen to filter western sun, reducing heat loads in the summer months. Can you explain the pattern content and how a viewer is meant to "read" this detail?

> This is a case where we took cultural information in the form of languages spoken in the neighborhood and organized them to drive a parametric model that generated a frit pattern. The generated pattern was an abstract representation of the languages and was combined with the word "SEARCH" translated into each of the languages to create a resonance for the viewers between something personal – the word in their own language – and something collective, which was the overall pattern created from all languages that form the community. There were 30 languages identified from census data that were grouped into four language groups. A horizontal bar represented each language and each group was made up of several bars stacked together to form a column, which appeared graphically like the spine of a book. Multiple versions of this "book," each representing a language group, were combined together to form the overall pattern reminiscent of books on shelves. The word SEARCH was translated into each of the languages and appears next to the "books" at eye level. Although it is a technical detail, the model allowed us to control the pattern where each language (and its representative bar) appears precisely in proportion to the number of people who speak that language in the community. For us, this was an exploration of how to use the quantitative precision of data to create a qualitative effect tied to the community, the building and the individual user.

The word "SEARCH" is projected by the sunlight through letters in the film in the parapet onto the glass curtain wall, varying in scale and legibility as a result of the time of day, degree of sunlight, and season. For a firm like yours that is fully engaged with technology in the design process, do you see this wall as a low-tech effect that explores the relationship between artifice and nature?

It is really not even low-tech. For this particular detail, there was a conscious decision to do something "no-tech." Our thinking was that it be simple in its execution and delivery. Originally we just wanted the sun to project the word "search" on the façade, but after studying it through simulations and large physical models we realized it was going to have many interesting effects over time, like the letters stretching in the summer and compressing in the winter due to the sun angle. The most powerful effect is when it is partly cloudy and the word literally pulsates on the building as the sun goes in and out of clouds. This was a case study in reducing the design down to the fewest number of components necessary to get the greatest effects. And in this case, it happens simply through seasonal variation and changes in the weather. It was really not an intellectual (i.e., culture and artifice) pursuit, but instead a pragmatic approach that cost very little and required no maintenance.

How much of your design work generates from any of these space-defining elements or components (as placeholders, originators, or borrowers)? Can cultural aspects, either explicitly or not, be embedded within a component?

I think cultural meaning can become part of the information in Building Information Modeling and this is a tremendous opportunity for architects to counter the current tendency of BIM to turn architecture into a product-driven design process. With the growth of manufacture-specific SmartBim components, design can become a kind of shopping list process, not unlike the days of Sweets Catalogues. Although these components can be parametric and allow users access to some inputs, they are still constrained by the information, or parameters, embedded by the manufacturer. Taken to an extreme, this tendency could lead to a point where design becomes almost an autonomous process where clients could download all of the components of a building, customize them to their needs through the limited inputs provided by the manufacturer and never need an architect. Several years ago, I had a conversation with a VP of a large software company who was predicting a similar scenario where, in the near future, the AEC industry would be centered on product manufacturers and they would be the largest employer of architects. Our ambitions as architects to embed cultural significance within the process, the components, and buildings need to be positioned in the context of these larger structural shifts occurring in industry.

Glen Oaks Library façade (image courtesy of Marble Fairbanks, photo credit Eduard Hueber)

To what extent to you see a BIM extending beyond the life of its outcome? Are you currently incorporating BIM facilities maintenance on any projects through post-occupancy?

The use of BIM for post-occupancy building management has a lot of surface appeal to clients and we push it in some projects, often by educating a client or contractor about the potential uses of a model to track and manage the lifecycle of a building. Institutions are typically the best clients for this type of exploration because they have multiple buildings that need to be kept up and maintained. BIM is well-suited for this particular kind of application and it will inevitably become more common. Many institutional clients are currently resistant to this because it requires retraining their entire staff. This issue of retraining and retooling is a problem at all stages of a project, which makes it challenging to promote cutting-edge technology with engineers, contractors, or clients who are not invested in change. The resistance is more cultural than technological, which is why I suspect the big industry shifts will happen with the next generation.

Is liability alleviated by the BIM and/or its process that architects have assumed in the past?

The entire contractual and insurance structure within the industry is arguably one of the biggest obstacles to real change. Although there is some movement toward shared risk, shared reward agreements between design teams, builders, and owners, these are difficult to execute because it requires systemic adjustments within all of industry. The simple answer, which has been stated many times, is that architects need to take on more risk . . . but we have to get paid for it. The last time I was involved with any conversation about contracts in relation to BIM and greater industry collaboration, it was concerning that lawyers were driving the discussion, not architects. My sense is that design teams, fabricators, and contractors all want to work more closely together and leverage the integration

capabilities of BIM and other technologies, but contracts and insurance are getting in the way. One anecdotal story – I was working with a façade consultant recently and they told me about a large project they were doing with very advanced design and fabrication workflows where the design and engineering model was in 3D and was being used directly for fabrication. It was a great example of what is possible today. However, by contract, they also had to produce shop drawings even though the parts were being fabricated directly from the model. The cheapest way to do this was to outsource the shops to a company in India, which resulted in hundreds of pages of unnecessary drawings. Among the many ironies was that the parts were fabricated and being installed long before the shops were even completed. These types of contractually driven inefficiencies are indicators of why change is needed.

"Search" phenomena on Glen Oaks Library façade (image courtesy of Marble Fairbanks, photo credit Eduard Hueber)

What other conditions of data inquiry or collaboration (beyond structural and mechanical engineers) does Marble Fairbanks intend to develop for your design process in general?

Exploring new forms of collaboration is always on our "to do" list. It relates to our desire to remain a small firm but operate with the most technologically advanced design workflows. One way to do this is through collaboration with non-traditional consultants that do specific research and offer specific skills. For example, for the *Toni Stabile Student Center* at Columbia University's Graduate School of Journalism, we wanted to incorporate many digitally driven processes, so we worked with three design collaborators outside the office and had them each work on a different part of the project. We were able to expand the technical (and design) capacity of our office and through a rigorous digital exchange and compilation process, end up with a very rich design solution. We are very interested in cultivating this type of network practice so that when we want to explore a technical process beyond the expertise of our office, we can work with other like-minded collaborators. This gives us a very agile capability to assemble a team on a per project basis. Often all this non-traditional collaboration work is invisible to the client (i.e., unbillable), which might raise certain liability issues, but that's what you have to do to overcome the limitations of a conventional practice. You have to stick your neck out to make progress.

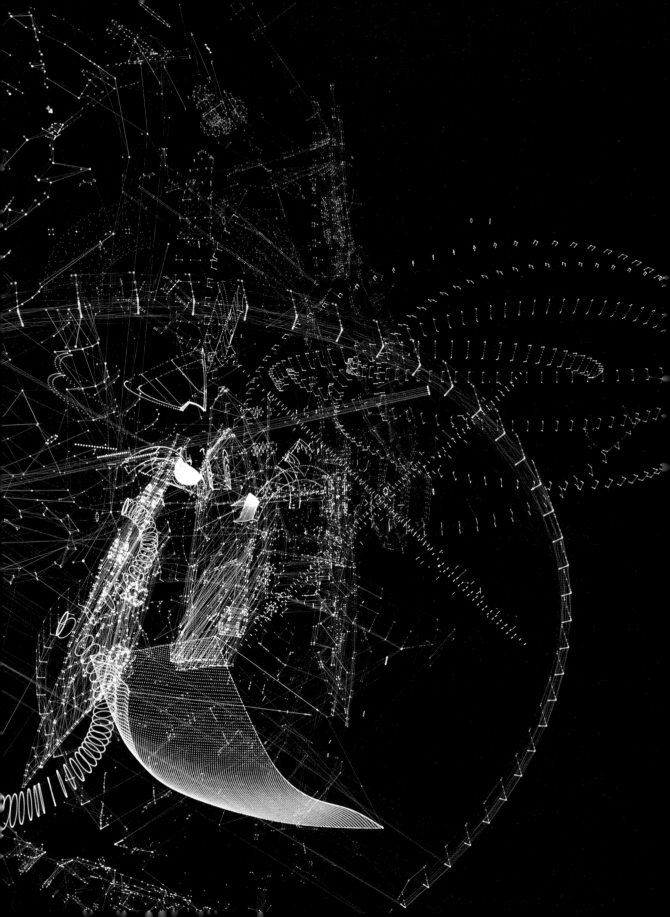

3

Point taken

When paying for groceries, every item in the basket gets scanned. Checking out a library book, the scan records when it is checked out and when it should be returned. Taking an airline flight, your checked bag is scanned so as to not end up in the wrong location – but if it does get lost, the scan tells the airline exactly where the bag is located. Scanning is common and critical and will soon become a much more advanced and incorporated part of daily life. A scan of the most basic pricing barcode on every item in a retail store provides simple product meta-data. Other forms of scanning – emerging out of new technologies – can capture billions of data points stored on millions of servers around the world, describing every facet of the real world. Defined by X, Y, and Z coordinates, these data point collections are intended to represent a three-dimensional coordinate system where the external surface of an object has spatial implications to consider. Artists and theorists have historically explored the complexity that can result from form made up of points. As seen in *A Sunday Afternoon on the Island of La Grande Jatte*, the French painter Georges Seurat's method of painting dot-by-dot empowered a single point – its size, position, color – to create unique visual effects reciprocal with the points around it. In a similar way, the direct feed of data points into a BIM URL can create "new geometry," capable of depicting alternative visualizations that reference energy audits, heritage site documentation, building analysis, or even more obscure physicality drawn from raw data.[1]

The hardware associated with BIM scanning is as readily available as the mobile phone camera and has become increasingly more common in an architect's toolset. The barcode tag creates BIM content instantaneously. This association allows an ongoing and reciprocal relationship between the designer and the products she uses. The constellation of previously hidden, but now discoverable, data implicates the design environment, and in the end creates a unique perceptual space within BIM.

Point cloud experimentation with graphical effects program, *Plexus* (image courtesy of Neil St. John, University of Greenwich, Postgraduate Diploma in Architecture, Instructor Nic Clear)

Graphic code

A barcode provides automated identification and data collection. Although its inception in 1952 facilitated labeling railroad cars, barcode technology was not truly accepted until scanners were developed in the 1970s. Today there are over five billion products that are scanned and tracked worldwide every day in this manner.[2] There are several kinds of barcodes in use today, including the standard Universal Product Code (UPC), more recently developed Quick Response (QR) codes, and the graphically enhanced Snap-tags. While the one-dimensional (1D) barcode has always provided basic product information (like price and description), it now also offers (through mobile application services) the ability to display geospatial purchasing locations, inventory management, tracking system direction, and user reviews. The graphically composed set of guard bars and number sequences link an increasingly vast record of information to an individual item in space and time. Newer forms of two-dimensional (2D) matrices, like QR codes, allow standard camera phones to scan points that link to several different types of data, including URL addresses (websites), phone numbers, and text messages. High capacity color barcodes (HCCBs) are the newest edition of 2D scanning codes. These offer greater flexibility than older formats in their ability to further the depth of data embedded in a single reference point through grids of colored triangles. Unlike earlier or more common barcodes, these tag codes deliver a more robust online experience and link to entire interactive mobile websites – thus user analytics are being reciprocally tracked behind the scenes for tag producers as well. More advanced scientific research offers multi-dimensional control through the point itself, using a color-tunable magnetic material and a lithographic printing method.[3] Using vivid, free-floating structural and colored particles, the magnetic micro-points have coding capacity easily into the billions, with distinct magnetic handling capabilities that include active positioning for code readouts and active stirring in micro-scale environments.[4]

In their application to BIM, the use of graphic UPCs, QR codes, and HCCBs lay out slight but meaningful differences. BIM, as an object-oriented, product-driven database, can schedule all the UPC codes of a project's building elements – even tracking their delivery to a job site.[5] When QR codes are posted at different physical locations on a project site or in the design documents, they can lead a scanner to the corresponding website or events of the project or products. They also sanction a project's

UPC barcode, QR code, and color-barcoded magnetic micro-particles (image rights by Danelle Briscoe, final figure provided by Rights Managed by Nature Publishing Group, © 2010)

2 3 9 6 6 3 2 4 6

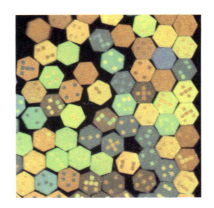

designer to reciprocally know all sorts of interesting things about the people scanning the code. Russia's futuristic pavilion at the 2012 Venice Architecture Biennale, designed by SPEECH, covered every bit of surface of a dome with giant QR codes that, when scanned, unleashed for visitors the plans and models for Skolkovo, a developing Russian city dedicated to science and technology. This technology is important not only in its implication for the transfer of knowledge in a new way, but more so the potential of space nesting into space by way of simple graphic points. HCCBs are not necessarily a huge leap forward, but do offer a graphic way to embed more data of a project, like the difference in capability between a compact disk and a memory stick for storing information. Now that the barcode has evolved, a system of magnetic color particles offers a speculative future for the production and degree of control offered by a point. This involves the cooperative action of magnetic ink and photo-curable resin, or spatiotemporally controlled ultraviolet exposure not unlike the 3D printing fabrication movement. A scalable version controlled from a barcoded BIM environment brings design down to the scale of the point.

Russia's 2012 Venice Biennale Pavillion (photo credit © Patricia Pavinejad)

Point collection

Spatial scanning, like the barcode scan of products, has a similar but inverse relationship to architectural design. Traditional site surveying, which used to be just rudimentary extrapolation of spatial information between two known points, relied on analog angle, distance measurement instruments, and the accuracy or disposition of the surveyor. Current scanning technology, known as LiDAR (light detection and ranging), records the amount of light bouncing off of objects and structures. The light emitted hits any object within a 360° range (which can be over a mile in some scans) and then creates incremental points to form a collection of what is known as a point cloud. A vector-based network places each point of the cloud within an X–Y–Z coordinate. More so, nested attributes like time, flight line, intensity (how much light comes back from a point), and color reside in each point. In this way, point clouds have their own physical characteristics separate from real-world data – a transferal that associates the physical world with the virtual one of BIM. The point cloud capture process offers an accurate and increasingly fast method for creating a complex model to input into a BIM environment. The accuracy of the scan indicates detail down to

the most subtle folds in a couch cushion. The points distinguish earth, water, buildings, roads, trees, crops, and countless other kinds of surface materials by their relationship to the light beam interaction. Such well-established precision makes this surveying process well matched for as-built documentation, as well as exploratory analysis or design.[6]

Particularly when dealing with real-world data sets, such detailed documentation of inhabitation can pose both challenges and advantages for designers. The example by Scot Page Architects of *Apartment 1204* in San Francisco displays the messy everyday-ness of exterior and interior spaces, with their cluttered and complex room shapes and content.[7] Paradoxically, the sheer size of the data file relays the enormity of information accuracy gathered and usually renders processing the data in core memory infeasible. Then again, the desire to capture and design for the minutiae of everyday life using dimensions beyond the third is evocative. The question of how much data is too much data is one that BIM proponents and critics ask repeatedly. The point cloud of a single building may easily consist of tens of gigabytes of data but at the same time can supply a narrative that other forms of documentation overlook. And if that scan were able to read all the product barcodes within the space and the meta-data they hold, the degree of difficulty or design control of building information would increase exponentially. Although such scanning is criticized in some circles for missing broader (potentially more critical) information, such as subsurface soil or water conditions, the process proves to be accurate at capturing usable and reliable configurations from the scale of a small intimate apartment to that of urban-scale civil structures.[8]

In terms of representation, the point capture has an inherent cone of vision (much like a camera lens aperture) requiring a project to be thoroughly scanned from multiple viewpoints. Piecing these vantage files together in a BIM platform then allows for multiple unified views. Surprisingly, when many point views are brought into a single scene, they start to show new qualities. Yet, the information for each capture contains (like a photograph) partial and dependent viewpoints. Trees, cars, and other peripheral elements can obscure the focus of the scan, but in the amalgamated point cloud, such obstructions can be orbited or made transparent for improved visualization.

The three-year European research project *Durable Architectural Knowledge* (*DURAARK*) focuses on the process of creating meaningful architectural information from point cloud data and linking it to BIM.

Apartment 1204 Mason St. (image provided by Scott Page Architects)

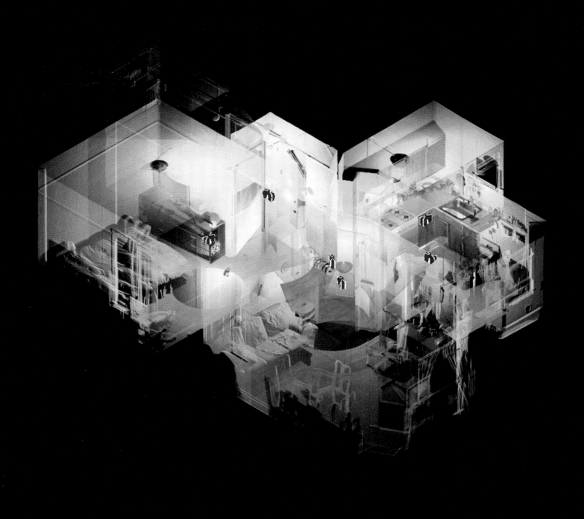

The work seeks to develop a methodology for relationships between the expanding field of architectural representations in BIM, point clouds, and geo-referenced data from web and images. One of the directors of the program, Martin Tamke from the Center for Information Technology and Architecture (CITA), claims "a real lifecycle of building related information is emerging, where a model from design stage has a meaning and impact on a building in its state of post-occupancy."[9] Currently, the rationale to use models in design does not often extend beyond construction into other stages, including facilities maintenance, where typically institutional building owners have a strong interest in final control of the long-term capabilities of a building and its digital representations.

DURAARK investigates how information can be retrieved from a single model or across a range of architectural representations. In a prototypical workflow developed by CITA and computer scientists at the University of Bonn, discrete 3D scans of a building can be automatically registered to each other, while an algorithmic approach segments the millions of 3D points into architectural entities, such as walls or doors, and detects objects like furniture. Everything that is detected can be translated into an Industry Foundation Class (IFC) model, an open and neutral BIM format. The concise description of each room, the objects it contains, its neighbors, and the spatial relationships between them provide novel relational information about a building's topology – allowing for new means by which to understand and assess architectural data. Instant searches for building substructures or objects within spaces can be performed on the extracted representation of the room connectivity. This process provides information for basic tasks, such as area and volume calculations, needed for the integration of existing buildings into facility management. As the 3D registration of architectural spaces becomes faster and widely accessible, a constant 3D monitoring of buildings becomes feasible – potentially allowing for the continuous optimization and adaptation of buildings to their users. Hence, Tamke sees the need for a conceptual extension of the design space into the realm of building operation. Methods like those developed by *DURAARK* will help to establish and extend links between diverse forms of information, including representations of spatial hierarchies, geometries, and design concepts in BIM; real world spaces; and to information about a building and its context online.

Algorithmic method for a semantic linkage of real-world spaces and their representation in BIM (image provided by the Center for Information Technology and Architecture, the Royal Danish Academy of Fine Arts, Schools of Architecture, Design and Conservation, Associate Professor Martin Tamke)

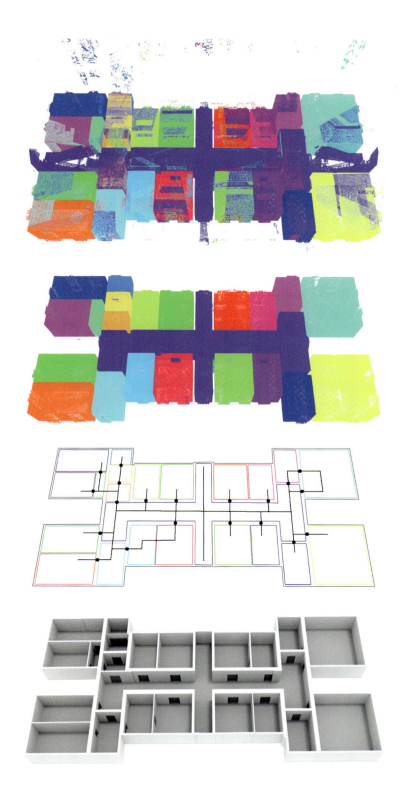

Dynamic point

Architects and engineers have at their disposal a variety of technologies available for sensing a person's location, behavior, and activity. Simple electronic beam-breakers positioned in strategic locations fire when a person crosses their path, tracking not only immediate movement, but also data points stored in that person's smartphone. Data can also be gathered on unwitting visitor behavior via video analytics, sensors inside ever-present mobile phones, and closed-circuit television (CCTV) that monitors point-to-point action for surveillance in high-security areas like banks, casinos, or airports. Unlike a barcode, these techniques of data gathering do not necessarily need to be within the line of sight of the reader, and may be embedded in the tracked object.

A point can assist with real-time decision-making – based on the timely location, activity, and behavior of actual human beings. SMART Space, a division of the world-renowned engineering firm BuroHappold, has developed a simulation platform called "Smart Move" that uses a combination of occupancy sensing, data visualization, and predictive behavior analysis to not only optimize design but also find ways of potentially choreographing user interaction and face-to-face contact. During the design phase of the *Louvre Abu Dhabi Museum*, Ateliers Jean Nouvel utilized the "Smart Move" technology to reveal how humans might interact under the 180-meter diameter lattice cupola. As a provocation for such a large space, one of the stated design objectives by Nouvel was to emphasize the generation of rare encounters.[10] According to Shrikant B. Sharma, Associate Director of the "Smart Move" research team, the simulation of such human happenstance furthered their research on predictive modeling and virtual testing of building spaces on the basis of the tracked data. Like known human responses to other stimuli in a particular type of space, avatars were used in the BIM environment as their real life counterparts.[11] The ability to use BIM as a "gaming space" by populating it with behavior points shows the application of point adaptation to the design process. Changes can be made in the 3D model by testing avatars' reactions to spatial proportion and issues like signage, fire, or overcrowding. These data can inform the strategic placement of programs by determining how many turns a person has to make to get from point A to B, or by counting footfalls in order to calculate the calorie expenditure of users. Each avatar in a simulation scenario acts as a dynamic reference point, much like a point's capacity in a "point cloud." By generating information for each potential person, the avatar specifically accounts for that individual's behavior over space and time.

The Louvre Abu Dhabi Museum, designed by Ateliers Jean Novel utilizing "Smart Move" technology (image provided by BuroHappold)

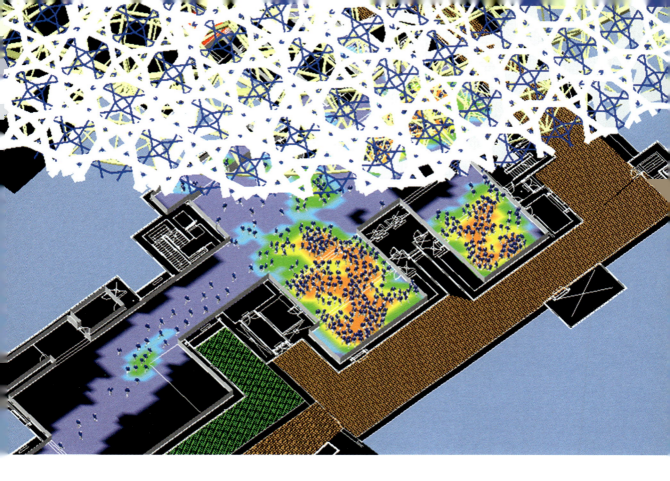

The process of converting data into a point cloud format cannot be assumed as a single trajectory of simply scanning existing space. Projects such as the *BMW Ball Bearing Kinetic Sculpture* and *HypoSurface* by the Mark Goulthorpe/dECOi office have explored the potential of parametrically driven, motorized agendas that exert individual control over every point of a surface. A more novel approach by James Leng, a Los-Angeles based Architect and Researcher, as seen in his project *Point Cloud*, plays off its titular term by reimagining daily interaction with weather through the physical exploration of a dynamically loaded point network. In the form of a cloud, each intersection point and node is flexibly driven by an Arduino connected to a thin wire frame. Arduino, as an open-source electronics platform, enables the interactive springs and wire's constant and chaotic motions to parse weather input/output data. The Arduino wireless module receives a constant data stream from public forecast centers like the National Oceanic and Atmospheric Administration. As a nebulous point system, *Point Cloud* is both precise and abstract, formed and formless, shifting between expansion and contraction. Instead of displaying static values for temperature, humidity, or precipitation, the project literally gyrates to the data it is fed.

The Arduino processors, along with 100 meters of cable and 966 joining points, result in an abstract visual interpretation of the various climate and weather parameters – points that will one day respond to live data streaming and potentially give details of gathering, incorporating, designing, and building. Where BIM favors objects with a defined, constrained relationship, Leng imagines using a physical information model to create unpredictable effects, letting inaccuracies build until something unexpected happens. For Leng, current BIM is a production tool, not a design tool. In his opinion, parametric tools have matured to a point where architects/designers are no longer entranced by the promise of a "design revolution."[12] Instead, he feels, users understand that BIM is an incredible tool for the process of *making*, but not necessarily for the process of thinking. Leng concludes, "At the risk of being very black and white, the design of fabrication rather than a building asks 'what' and 'why', while BIM answers the question of 'how'. But it is so often the 'how' that brings a project to life."[13]

Point Cloud Arduino detail (image provided by James Leng)

Conclusion

Once considered disruptive, the scanning process has found a settled but speculative position in architecture. With technologies like "Smart

Move" and BIM emerging in parallel, the ability has now arrived to visualize data spatially, and in real time. The case studies presented in this chapter investigate the types of information that are necessary for design, and they provide methods for controlling the appropriate level of information intake. The notion of hyper-exactitude meeting metaphysical erasure signifies a shift within the BIM environment – one that will continue to transform architecture in its building and contextual effects. In his lecture "It's All About Particles," architect Enric Ruiz Geli claims that "Le Corbusier's buildings were about skin, but the new language of architecture is driven by particles."[14] This position envisions a not-so-distant future where the barcode, with its inherent complexity and flexibility, may be able to do all manner of amazing things for architecture: assist project installation and instructions, allow for stakeholder feedback, and facilitate project information in innovative ways.

Point Cloud in space (image provided by James Leng)

Notes

1. Scott Page, email to the author, June 19, 2014.
2. Stuart Smith, "Say Goodbye to a Bar Code Legend," *Mintek* (December 17, 2012), www.mintek.com/blog/cpe-management/goodbye-bar-code-legend.
3. Hyoki Kim, Jianping Ge, Junhoi Kim, Sung-Eun Choi, Hosuk Lee, Howon Lee, Wook Park, Yadong Yin, and Sunghoon Kwon, "Structural Colour Printing Using a Magnetically Tunable and Lithographically Fixable Photonic Crystal," *Nature Photon* 3 (2009): 534–540.
4. Lee Howon, Junhoi Kim, Hyoki Kim, Jiyun Kim, and Sunghoon Kwon, "Colour-Barcoded Magnetic Microparticles for Multiplexed Bioassays," *Nature Materials* 9 (2010): 745–749.
5. Jesse Reiser and Nanako Umemoto, *Atlas of Novel Tectonics* (Princeton, NJ: Princeton Architectural Press, 2006).
6. Scott Page offers a detailed explanation of the use of LIDAR for as-built documentation and translation into BIM ["3D Laser Scanning: As-Built Reality Capture for BIM," *AECbytes Viewpoint* 66 (November 29, 2012)]. Page explains how the scanning and post-processing took a day, the BIM model was built from the scan data that night (by architecture graduate student, Sarah Bonser), and another team did the energy audit from the model. It was all delivered later as a "challenge" sponsored by Autodesk, FARO, and Pacific Gas and Electric to illustrate the power of new technologies.
7. The University of Wisconsin-Madison's Wisconsin Institute of Discovery project "vizHOME" creates a context-based information needs assessment strategy, which uses clutter and chaos to uncover health issues for medical purposes. Others, like Assistant Professor Benjamin Ibarra at the University of Texas at Austin School of Architecture, use the technology to map and uncover structural meaning of historical Spanish gothic arches in Mexico.
8. Philip Belesky, email to the author, July 28, 2014.
9. Martin Tamke, interview with the author, October 23, 2014.
10. Alison Furuto, "The Louvre Abu Dhabi Museum, Ateliers Jean Nouvel," *ArchDaily* (November 26, 2012), www.archdaily.com/298058/the-louvre-abu-dhabi-museum-ateliers-jean-nouvel.
11. Shrikant Sharma, email to the author, July 28, 2014.
12. James Leng, email to the author, July 8, 2014.
13. Ibid.
14. Enric Ruiz Geli, "It's All About Particles," lecture at Autodesk University Design Computation Symposium, Las Vegas, Nevada, December 2, 2013.

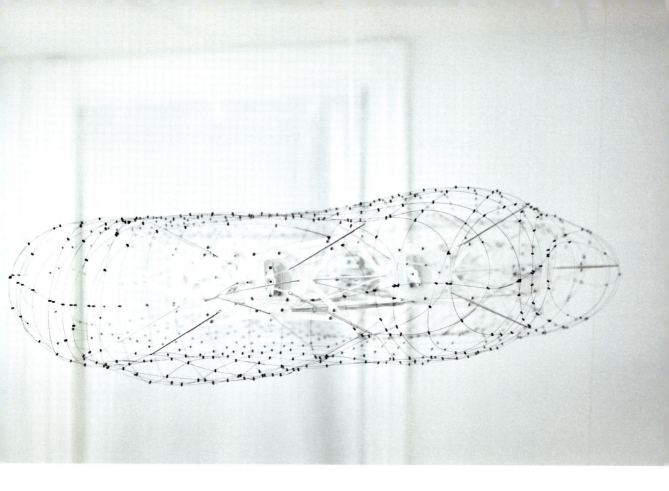

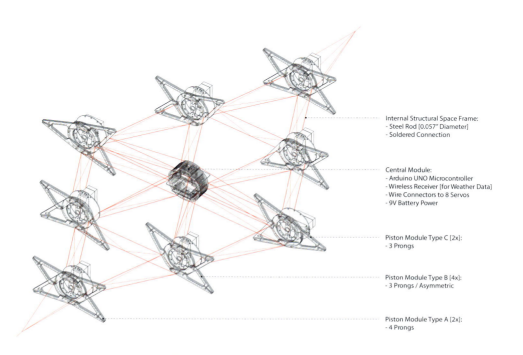

Internal Structural Space Frame:
- Steel Rod [0.057" Diameter]
- Soldered Connection

Central Module:
- Arduino UNO Microcontroller
- Wireless Receiver [for Weather Data]
- Wire Connectors to 8 Servos
- 9V Battery Power

Piston Module Type C [2x]:
- 3 Prongs

Piston Module Type B [4x]:
- 3 Prongs / Asymmetric

Piston Module Type A [2x]:
- 4 Prongs

[INTERVIEW]

Elena Manferdini
ATELIER MANFERDINI

BIM techniques have gained the reputation of being a directive toward more normative conditions of form creation, and to some extent provoking a more restrained approach to architectural design. Has BIM (or data-driven process in general) enabled or inhibited your design process?

When I think of BIM, I imagine an office that has a workflow that is geared toward building and coordinating many contractors and industries that need a way to communicate. I would put myself in that group of architects that are not yet at that level of practice – where the concern for information and the ability to share it with many contractors is a main focus. In my office the most interesting workflow is the one we use to translate three-dimensional design into bi-dimensional information and back to fully volumetric construction. During the phase when volumes become flat, something interesting takes place: flatness has the ability to proliferate at multiple scales into numerous fabrication techniques and into a variety of materials. Flatness is where fine arts, graphic design, architecture, and painting can coexist onto one abstract plane. Suddenly, there is no more camera eye perspective, there's no hierarchy, it's not real materiality . . . it's a very powerful moment. In my practice we are much more engaged with how to use digital design tools to be creative and to find novel aesthetic output, rather than deploying computers for data input. Specifically in my office, when we work with other offices we adopt BIM to be able to share files and communicate. It is clear that the industry is moving toward BIM. We are currently working on a large mixed-use project in Los Angeles for LA County called *San Fernando Valley Family Center*, we have been asked to design the interior lobby space, a portion of the curtain wall, and a partial garden design. We are using BIM to interface with the main project architect and consultants. Usually we work with other 3D modeling platforms (specifically *Rhino*,

Out of Focus, four panels of 4 × 8 feet each (1" thick), May 2014, COLA fellowship, Los Angeles County Arts Commission for the future San Fernando Valley Family Support Center (image courtesy of Atelier Manferdini)

Tempera, "A New Sculpturalism: Contemporary Architecture From Southern California," Geffen Contemporary, The Museum of Contemporary Art, Los Angeles, June 2012–September 2013 (image courtesy of Atelier Manferdini)

Maya, *Zbrush* and *Grasshopper*) and *Processing*. For graphic design creation, we often use 3D scanning as a point of departure. Because of the amount of polygons produced by 3D scanning, with current technology it is hard to link the data we scan to a database to control it.

Do you see BIM as being antithetical to generative design and building in innovative ways for the discipline in general?

I think BIM is a necessity. It is actually a way to define information, add intelligence to geometry, maintain control and create systems, but it has yet to contain the intelligence of materials or the design fluidity that designers aim to have. It's a great tool, but it is not comprehensive for the creative design phases of a project. I don't think BIM is antithetical to creation, but it does require a lot of acceptance of convention in order to input geometry. And therefore, a lot of users actually are responding to that workflow. It asks questions of a designer that are maybe too early to ask sometimes. When you are drawing the first line in the computer, you may not know what kind of wall it is yet.

Often a designer needs some time before being able to get to a point where one really need BIM to control it. I imagine building models in one software and then swapping them into another, and then modeling them again can be effective in making those decisions, but with the downside of time consumption. Probably in offices whose work is very repetitive going directly into BIM is efficient because they know exactly what kind of evaluation they are looking for. But design is quicksand and it's labor intensive.

Can you describe your 3D translation process and what source of information you use?

My design process in the last four years has focused on other techniques, like 3D scanning and more painterly tools like *Zbrush* that actually completely change the way we think about making models. For many years, I was making 3D models using abstract rules to code repetitive routines. That created a certain level of complexity and, in a sense, order in the work. That became uninteresting after a while, so four years ago I changed my process and went to an analog source of information, like 3D-scanning existing objects.

So you make an object and then you scan it?
No, I just scan. I scan objects – that is, mostly still nature work – insects, animals, flowers and trees. That process is the first step in surface manipulation and becomes either a 2D graphic or enlaced with different materials. There is always a reference to the real. My goal is to promote an imbalance quality where you might wonder what things are and where they come from. It has a new tactile material quality but a familiar DNA. A majority of the work I do comes from these found objects to completely go against the idea of abstract geometry and systems that trigger multiple layers of connections. Like any design, where you can choose to be as abstract or figural, my current work is tending primarily to figural. I work from the point cloud of those objects and start manipulating geometry, aesthetics, and materiality where the surface finish is of primary consideration. Really, I am consciously trying to make the process a bit more intuitive and exploiting what the computer cannot do. Particularly now with coding, there is a certain synthetic quality to things – an outcome your eyes can always immediately find. I have found that using analog materials to generate suddenly subverts the intelligence. Also, the software allows me to work more sculpturally. As with *Zbrush*, the 3D object can be cut and painted which is what I am doing with most of my time.

Is this process at the scale of the building or for a particular project?
At the scale of the surface. The skin is the datum and is always the wrapper to go from 2D to 3D, and I work on both in a systematic way. Not in the same way that BIM might imply alliance to a datum. The geometry is unfolded and my alliance is to that 2D materiality. Mainly creating the dimensional painting of a surface and three-dimensional volume for the elements. There is depth to the graphic, there is depth to the painting, and there is depth to the architectural surfaces. It's still surface application whether it is an inlay of materials or a print. It is still surface quality with three-dimensionality but then flattened, or very thin. Or you could say it's

thick-ish. But it currently occupies building-scale surface of spaces, even if those elements come from other architects.

I know that you use BIM when you collaborate with others, but in your own work (where you say you are not using BIM), how do you quantify or schedule the parts and pieces?

In a very labor-intensive, manual way (tabular spreadsheet and some visual programming). We are creatures of habit. You know, you get used to doing things a certain way and change is not always easy. My desire to learn any new software (like *Zbrush* or *Processing*) is to create new work, not to document it. After a while you don't really want to do shop drawings, you want to have a big enough budget for the contractor to do the shop drawings, even if they will never be as good as when you do them yourself. As soon as they do the shop drawings and there is a problem, you can point to the problem and define responsibility. If you produce a 3D BIM model then you are responsible and liable. In the *Hubert Humphrey Los Angeles Health Care Facility*, my office produced all the BIM models for fabrication and estimation. We decided to keep it in the office because the budget was very limited, and I wanted the experience of creating the BIM for fabrication and I wanted the confidence to know that it would be done right. That is not worthwhile because in a traditional contract structure, I then become liable for everything. When you have multiple people overlapping in a model, it becomes questionable who is responsible for errors even when it was another collaborator's decisions. So I have learned that actually it is better to contract out the quantity and schedule items, unless the work is incredibly complex and you really are the only one who can produce that model. Creating separate 3D models and letting others be liable eliminates the single database document heated legal path. The ability for a contractor to point at your model and ask for change orders is so much greater than if they are given 2D construction documents..

Do you consider any post-construction life of a model, like maintenance or life-cycle?

I'm working on three public projects and I have all sorts of design review requirements by Los Angeles County to analyze for issues of

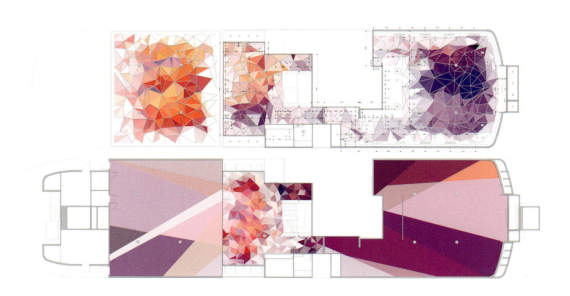

Bianca, Lake Biwa, Japan 2012, interior and exterior renovation of a 60 m cruise boat, Keihan Group (image courtesy of Atelier Manferdini)

how things will be maintained for the next 25 years. No contractor, no fabricator, no paint manufacturer can achieve the expectation of the 25-year standard that LA County expects. The consultant goes through our material list and assembly and points out possible conflicts or problems. At that point, I have already gone through most of the problems, but I still have to contact all the fabricators and get warranties for all the materials. It is a lot of leg work. And if something does not already have a warranty – for example I am working with a very atypical ceramic that falls into this scenario – I'm going to have to test it to meet the code requirements. So anytime you go beyond what the commercial fabricator is currently doing, you have to prove it, which is time consuming and expensive.

Although you have fabulous work at multiple scales, is the building really the ultimate goal?

My first degree was not in architecture so I have been exposed to architects in Italy that design anything from the scale of an object to a building and that flexibility is part of their strength and everyone does it. It affords a particular kind of efficiency. I think the specialization that I definitely see in the United States might not be present in the figure of the architect in Europe. I do enjoy very much all the types of projects I do and I think of them all as architectural projects no matter what scale. Generally speaking, others I know who are truly creative people, transcend (either by necessity, curiosity or desire) this role as designers, thinkers, collaborators, educators, and surround themselves with like-minded people from all disciplines at many scales.

OVERLEAF
Out of Focus detail, four panels of 4 × 8 feet each (1″ thick), May 2014, COLA fellowship, Los Angeles County Arts Commission for the future San Fernando Valley Family Support Center (image courtesy of Atelier Manferdini)

4
Environmental fact or fiction

In the 1920s, modern architects addressed environmental welfare with available technology: air-conditioning units and updated mechanical systems. The attitude reflected in Reyner Banham's seminal text *The Architecture of the Well-Tempered Environment* characterized the discipline's urge to engage these new technological developments implicitly through form and space. Banham described the timely intentions for a technologically serviced form as "attractive enough for its rents to absorb the 8% cost increase for air-conditioning, fluorescent lighting and acoustical dropped ceilings." By that time, architects had more or less accepted that their post-war skyscraper dreams were to be realized in a stark orthogonal and rectilinear aesthetic.[1]

The Information Age is now reaching a youthful maturity.[2] With Android device in hand, architecture continues to celebrate the first machine age while grappling with formal exploration afforded by an economy based on information computerization. Moreover, BIM creates a crossroads between environmental factors and design/formal choices as either authentically based on real-time data (fact) or arbitrarily derived from aesthetic concerns or narrative (fiction). Adherence to and allocation of environmental factors (now coded as data) further antagonize this relationship of design decision making to either be subservient to the information, to selectively manipulate it or to disregard these factors as a willful play of fictional narrative. Straightforward, embedded capabilities, such as simulation, analysis and collaboration in BIM, renegotiate the formal critical split into many instances. Unlike Banham's singular solution to form in relation to technology, a compliance to environmental data results in any number of formal solutions; searching for a balance of optimized relationship between data and form. In the end, is this actually a fulfillment of Banham's larger idea of the well-tempered environment?

The idea that form – simply by its shape and position on the planet – can generate its own self-sustaining efficiency and positive energy flow through and around a building is a very traditional strategy

Data.tron, audiovisual installation at Deep Space venue. Composition: Ryoji Ikeda; programming: Tomonaga Tokuyama. Ars Electronica Center, Linz, AT, W16 × H9 × D9 m, 2008–2009 (image courtesy of Ryoji Ikeda, photo by Liz Hingley © Ryoji Ikeda)

Early *Solar Envelopes* on Downtown Los Angeles, Ralph Knowles' Solar Studio at University of Southern California (image courtesy of Ralph Knowles)

for environmental control. As architects now have the ability to quantify (and inevitably qualify) beneficial information at greater depth and volume, innovative equipment and hardware can also strategically improve a building's post-construction comfort state and the potential to educate a building's users (and the discipline at large) on energy usage and service. Often categorized as either passive or active systems, these agendas remain fundamental in terms of an environmental BIM approach. How do new BIM methods allow for a more integrated and reciprocal relationship between the two? A focus on passive form-making suggests the significance of geometry in the quest to balance aesthetic choices alongside energy efficiencies. BIM design, with its multitude of parts and pieces, enables new ways of addressing active environmental solutions and subsequently their dissemination.

Passive approach

Until recently, environmental information as common as solar, water, and wind conditions relied solely on physical analyses. To test, for example, the sun's impact on design form, an analog process requiring a physical model in a sun simulator, or *Heliodon*, was used. For more than 30 years, Ralph Knowles, Professor Emeritus at the University of Southern California, established this process through a project and term he coined the *Solar Envelope*. He defined the solar envelope on a given site as "the volumetric limits of building that control shadows on surroundings at specified times."[3] During the energy crisis of the 1970s, when Knowles first published his research, he prioritized analog sun-angle data as a way to maximize solar access when building in high-density areas, such as downtown Los Angeles. The physical model's information feedback turned what would have been a Banham-described rectilinear extrusion into slopes and projections that adhered to the environmental data from the sun. If data is an assumed asset in an environmental design agenda, then what does it now enable that Knowles' heuristic process overlooked?

Armed with BIM technologies, an environmental agenda inspires a multitude of approaches for a design workflow. In service to form, database capabilities can turn sun and wind profiles on or off like a switch, extend early-stage analysis, or even collect and reuse raw data to solve (or create) design problems. In this sense, solar conditions may remain abstract, but are informed with great specificity. Geometry

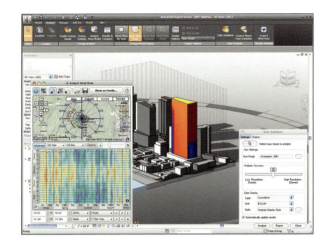

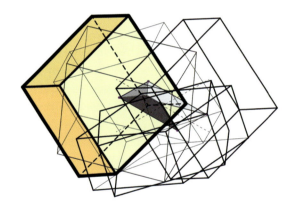

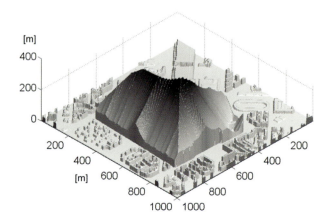

Top: BIM environmental support within creation space (Autodesk screenshots reprinted with the permission of Autodesk, Inc).* *Middle*: *BIM Solar Envelope* plug-in (image courtesy of Karen Kensek). *Bottom*: *Solarscape* plug-in (image courtesy of Eugenio Morello)

* Autodesk, Vasari registered trademarks or trademarks of Autodesk, Inc., and/or its subsidiaries and/or affiliates in the USA and other countries.

is no longer neutral in that it holds values according to the virtual environment of its exact geographic location. By using a direct and inclusive connection to Google Maps, site identity markers – a street address, nearest major city, latitude and longitude – can offer up interactive links of geospatial information to BIM. Location-specific shadows and predominant wind angles are based on weather station(s) within close range of almost any location on the planet. Geometry, then, responds to any time, day, or season within that environment allocation – information that in the end directly affects heating and cooling requirements. The shadow may be a fact, but the narrative opportunities to choreograph its path through form remains open to interpretation and implementation.

The ability to customize the BIM process with plug-ins offers additional means to investigate an interest like a solar design process. One such plug-in, also called *Solar Envelope*, expands upon Knowles' approach by defining virtual geometry as a dependent of both the BIM site and the sun's path.[4] The major difference with this plug-in research and development is its ability to work within BIM automation to explore multiple values for the spontaneous adjustments for quick iterations. Another equal but broader scaled approach refines the definition of the solar envelope to more accurately reflect the actual irradiation and illumination of the city. A new technique for urban analysis known as *Solarscape* simplifies solar envelope calculations, making them easier to carry out over extensive urban areas. Based on the image processing of the Digital Elevation Model (DEM), the use of an urban raster model operates as an underlay in BIM space. The DEM is shown to be "conducive to the environmental analysis of extensive urban areas" to further contribute to the assessment of radiative landscape in cities.[5] The consideration of building surface energy reduces the concept of "solar envelope" down to the scale of the component, as well as what can be embedded in BIM geometry. These tools, which take climate information over the last 20 years and project it onto the project site to calculate the degree of solar gain at any given hour, presumably feed data to prevent a designer from any bias or prejudice that might distort the ultimate meaning of the work in question. However, determining which facts to choose, or the depth at which to empower the data, can just as easily render intuitive, insufficient or incorrect information.

The Future House (image courtesy of Innovarchi)

Passive form

The current expectation is for architectural form to do more than just visually excite. In the same way that volume can be a result of legal prescriptions,[6] environmental data provide an authority over formal inherent subjectivity and returns the discipline to a condition of information-driven functionalism. Adolph Loos viewed architecture as an extension of nature, or "objects whose visual features seemed derived entirely from the physical functions they performed, just like a tree."[7] William McDonough and Michael Braungart, co-authors of *Cradle to Cradle: Remaking the Way We Make Things*, echoed that sentiment with their suggestion to model design in the likeness of a cherry tree. The practicalities of making architecture environmentally responsive (or like a tree) are, however, not so straightforward. Short of its tendency toward symbolic narrative or metaphor, architecture risks turning "building" into a meaningless way to cover space, like tilt-wall shopping centers and corrugated aluminum sheds.

Kostas Terzidis, Professor at Harvard Graduate School of Design and author of *Algorithmic Architecture*, argues for the importance of form over function and content – he argues for the fiction of tree-ness. His particular means of form generation utilize idiosyncratic computational links – links that can ultimately involve environmental factors. Those waving a flag for sustainability hold suspicious regard for such a formalist agenda, and as a consequence, continue to deem technological development of complex form as superficial.[8] Prior accusations of iconoclasm now fall short when data harvesting means a design is declared by the constraints of its information, rather than its shape.[9]

The *Future House*, by Innovarchi, is a small but powerful project that uses form to accommodate the Australian sun, wind, and water. Designed as a concept for the *Built Environment House of the Future Competition* in 2004, this affordable and innovative project highlights how a single-surface's passive geometry soaks up sunlight and rain in order to naturally heat and cool the interior space.

> We wanted to express the fact that a house of the future can be made with more flexible geometries through information based design and fabrication techniques. What was once thought to be expensive – changing sectional shape within one structure – is now affordable and feasible

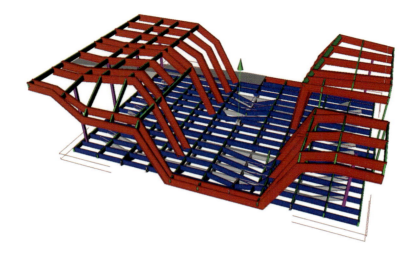

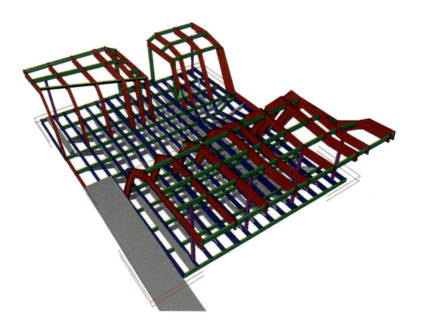

The Future House sectional models (image courtesy of Innovarchi)

explains Stephanie Smith, Design Director of Innovarchi.[10] Each prefabricated structural profile is unique and the concept is driven by the multi-functionality of the surface. The undulation creates internal and external spaces that promote new, less isolated possibilities for living. As the faceted roof becomes the ground of the courtyard between the two volumes of the house, the surface drains water into the center space without defaulting to the most basic flat skillion, or Australian shed, form.

The single surface combines commonly known building elements – typical and discrete BIM components such as floor, roof, and wall – into a single entity. The conflation of these elements in a BIM environment redefines the language of the default standards, which as a by-product leads to a particular data efficiency. In other words, instead of three object files, it is combined into one. Compiling the building elements into a single component reduces the visualization of discrete parts, but still allows each facet of the surface to be individually quantified for solar altitude, azimuth, direct and diffuse radiation driven from a climate file. The single surface is defined in terms of explicit sun or shadow hours, referencing actual radiation or illumination levels. All the while, the network of associations makes the model accessible and editable throughout. Finding the whole to be a literal sum of its parts allows for both design and functional flexibility.

Active education

On average, architects select 1,600 products and make over 17,000 decisions during the design and construction of a project.[11] Object models such as low-water toilets, solar panels, wind generators, recycling bins, and energy-efficient hand dryers already reside by default as files in the current BIM library under a "Sustainability" subfolder. As such, BIM plays an active role in the proliferation of these objects as well as the design of other active parts that embed meaning into what might otherwise be considered mundane. This raises the issue of whether the BIM process enhances a designer to forego design freedom for prescriptive selection of strategic parts and pieces. Is this training for innovation?

Driven by the desire to create a building that its users will directly learn from, the *Knox Innovation Training Opportunity and Sustainability Center* (*KIOSC*) showcases an array of active and passive systems that

 =

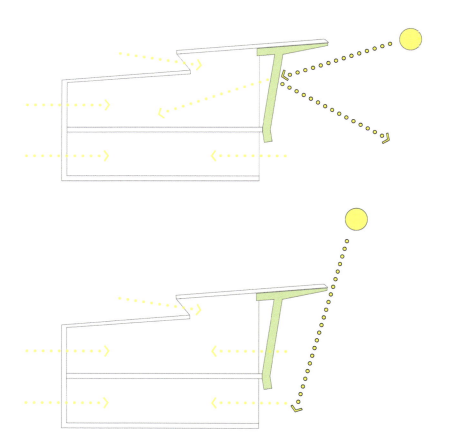

The *KIOSC* building element diagram (image courtesy of Woods Bagot)

ON PAGES 78–79
The *KIOSC* (courtesy of Woods Bagot, photo credit Peter Bennett)

are informed by the sun and engaged through technology. Designed by Woods Bagot of Australia in 2011, the deep northern eaves, glazing, and sun blades notably optimize the building's north and south façades and maximize natural light. Built as a training hub to prepare secondary-school students for careers in sustainability, the multiple vertical fins minimize direct solar loads, reduce glare, and visually promote (through varying shades of green) an environmental sensibility determined by a critically calculated sun angle. The unique façade comprises 36 undulating louvers and visually expresses its environmentally attuned origins, offering a creative and passive position to its active and explicit nature of data. "The blade wall is the focal point, but it also helps educate kids about sustainable building systems and construction through interactive learning," says Design Principal for the project, Bruno Mendes. Throughout the interior, touch screens describe the building's green initiatives and students can use cell phones or tablets to scan QR codes embedded on the façade to learn about the daily glazing performance and the building's energy efficiency as a whole.[12]

This project represents the transitional phase that many firms have experienced, where the majority of design consultants were using BIM tools, but at different stages, and for varying purposes. Mendes says this project went through their office when the firm was in the process of extending existing BIM processes toward parametric/computational design. When asked whether the structural and mechanical engineers' use of BIM enabled or inhibited their design work, Mendes' response was wholeheartedly, "BIM definitely made it easier to review and incorporate their models into our own design work."[13] The BIM workflow requires more upfront input, but reduces work in the cross check with consultant documentation and feedback. BIM creates the expectation that at certain project milestones, all issues and conventional documentation (plans, elevations, and drawings) are coordinated and integrated with the model.[14]

A particular collaborative space of BIM provides a system for measurement and verification directed toward an environmental agenda. Being in this collaborative circle affords access to its direct benefits, such as the instantaneous exchange, similar to that of an internet chat room, where everyone and their expertise are sitting around the virtual table, graphically designing and constructing a building model together. Sometimes this exchange is strictly among primary consultants – architecture, structural, or mechanical – while at other times (happening

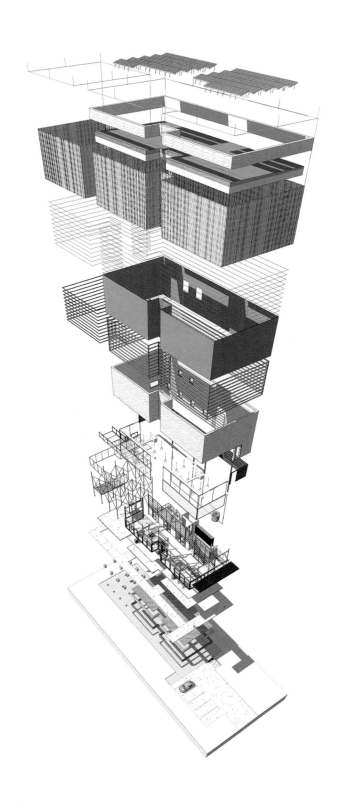

The *Ecohawks Research Facility* diagram (courtesy of Dan Rockhill & Studio 804)

ON PAGES 82–83
Ecohawks Research Facility student design/build installation of custom Aerogel-filled garage doors (image courtesy of Dan Rockhill & Studio 804)

more often than not), BIM collaborators have more specific goals of environmental fact, such as thermal analysis, to fertilize the design process of the building and thus affect the fiction of its form. Dan Rockhill, a distinguished Professor of Architecture at the University of Kansas School of Architecture, leads the legendary Studio 804 program each year. He heads up a 20-student design/build project with a twofold "build" studio agenda: incorporating the most active building elements afforded by industry, alongside the physical act of making a full-scale information-based building in KU's pre-construction workshop and then later on-site. Hunter Hanahan, one of Studio 804's 2013 veteran students, addresses standard BIM with: "Our studio felt that BIM would be the best approach to allow more of the team to move more efficiently through the documentation part of the process. There were times when 5 of us [students] were working in the single BIM project model at once."[15] Perhaps more significantly, the BIM process allowed for upfront strategies to develop between student BIM and environmental engineer via real-time simulation. According to Rockhill, "The students most definitely benefit with the use of BIM and are able to capitalize on some of the energy model information from the consultants through that platform."[16]

The Ecohawks, a student program run by the KU School of Engineering, focuses on alternative energy for transportation. Their *Ecohawks Research Facility*, Studio 804's 2013 design/build outcome, is one continuous structure split into three pods: two enclosed spaces for working on electric vehicles, and one open-air volume for outdoor research and learning. Although the rectangular geometry itself avoids iconicity, over 6,000 square feet of the exterior cladding is a woven aluminum, custom mesh system that appears to move and transform with the passing sun. Below the weave sits a glazed storefront system, which faces directly south for natural light and passively heats the interior during the winter months. The translucent panels are filled with Aerogel, an extremely efficient and lightweight thermal insulator. By using an inert gas like argon, the project was able to achieve higher insulation (U-value) properties compared to air. Since much of the envelope was glass and by default a primary driver of the building's heat load, it was critical to have this custom BIM element produce a net-zero (net positive) space as a load-reduction strategy. Ryan Evans, the Director of Sustainability for Henderson Engineers, Inc. and Lead Engineer collaborator for the project, believes the combination of BIM

with third-party analysis offered a measurement and verification strategy that defined inputs for both a baseline (code minimum) building and for the proposed construction.[17] The facility is designed to produce 12 percent more energy from its 14.5 kW photovoltaic array than it uses, which is fed back into the power grid. To add to the already innovative ways for teaching and building with BIM, such collaboration for sustainable strategies is incorporated throughout the building design and construction, and all contributed to the LEED Platinum Certification of this project.

Conclusion

Design has always responded to dynamic natural forces. The degree to which the discipline acknowledges these forces is, quite remarkably, no longer in flux. With certainty, a designer who chooses to disregard information so readily available in rate and magnitude leaves herself open to charges of negligence, whereas careful consideration of such information constitutes basic best practice. As the current technology supports and reinforces a less arbitrary desire for environmental responsiveness, this also raises questions of design freedom versus prescription. BIM makes it more difficult for the discipline to trump such metrics in pursuit of a purely narrative response, but also prompts, through its facility for minutia, a balance to the value-driven results from past practices. The creation of new form and space is afforded by virtual analysis and simulation.

The bigger question posed by Knowles (pre-CAD and pre-BIM) still proves relevant for the current predicament of data-to-design integration: can cities (and their buildings) be transformed by the use of environmental data in design? Does an ostensible data-optimized form necessarily equate to better quality of space or urban condition? Indeed, standard BIM techniques can guide form creation according to coinciding data-driven factors that not only eschew sculptural iconicity but also contradict the prevailing criticism of BIM – one that forces a more mechanical and less creative approach to building. Rather than viewing environmental fact and fiction as separate directions, their alignment embarks on an accountable design freedom. Perhaps more critical is the means by which the general public and future architects are both educated in understanding this alignment, either through their own studies or experience and engagement with actual buildings in the environment. The use of an advanced database technology like BIM accelerates the nature of applicable measures and accountability.

Notes

1. Reyner Banham, *The Architecture of the Well-Tempered Environment* (Chicago, IL: University of Chicago Press, 1984), pp. 182–183.
2. We are now two decades from when Nicholas Negroponte actually began to define a post-Information Age in *Being Digital* (New York, NY: Random House, 1995).
3. Ralph Knowles, *Sun Rhythm Form* (Boston, MA: MIT Press, 1981), p. 15.
4. Alicyn Henkhaus and Karen Kensek, "Solar Access Zoning + Building Information Modeling," talk delivered at SOLAR 2013, ASES's 42nd Annual National Solar Conference, Baltimore, MD, April 16–20, 2013.
5. Eugenio Morello and Carlo Ratti, "Sunscapes: 'Solar Envelopes' and the Analysis of Urban DEMs," *Computers, Environment and Urban Systems* 33, no. 1 (2009): 26–34.
6. New York City's Zoning Law of 1916 is emblematic as it forced a reaction against negative environmental effects caused by excessive building height and density on central Manhattan.
7. Rudolf Arnheim, *Dynamics of Architectural Form* (Berkeley, CA: University of California Press, 1978).
8. Kostas Terzidis, *Expressive Form: A Conceptual Approach to Computational Design* (New York, NY: Spoon Press, 2003), p. 9.
9. TEX-FAB Symposium Workshop, San Antonio, Texas, April 15, 2011, modeLAB Ronnie Parsons & Gil Akos.
10. Stephanie Smith, email to the author, June 2, 2014.
11. Sally Darling, Director of ESD Solutions of Australia, email to the author, May 29, 2014.
12. www.architectmagazine.com/walls/blades-of-green.aspx (retrieved December 14, 2014).
13. Bruno Mendes, Principal at Woods Bagot, email exchange with the author, September 14, 2014.
14. Woods Bagot, with BuroHappold Engineers, have since fully adopted BIM and have gone so far as to develop a BIM plug-in they call 'Zero Emissions Design' (ZERO-E). Their intention is to advance the construction industry's contribution to realizing a zero-carbon economy by 2050 and enable architects, in terms of interactive design, to autonomously track energy usage and carbon footprints for design solutions developed in BIM. This joint initiative is not only an entirely new model for environmental design, it is also a call to action for greater collaboration of development and construction partners.
15. Hunter Hanahan, email to the author, September 25, 2014.
16. Dan Rockhill, interview with the author, October 11, 2014.
17. For LEED projects, Studio 804 is required to use ASHRAE 90.1 – 2007 Appendix G Modeling Methodology, a comprehensive industry standard. This was achieved using a BIM methodology in combination with eQuest modeling software by Henderson Engineering.

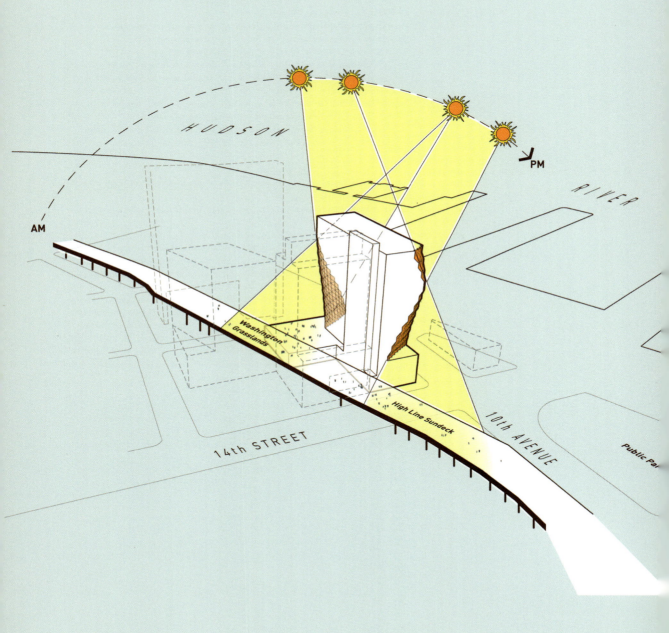

[INTERVIEW]

Jeanne Gang
STUDIO GANG ARCHITECTS

Has BIM or data-driven process in general enabled your design?

When I think about how technology can enable architecture design, I'm most excited by the implications of information, including user data, citizen science, and measuring performance. Technological advancements in the architect's drawing tools have changed the *how* of our craft, but the information revolution enabled by data has the potential to change *what* an architect does. Access to information will be the key to expanding the architect's role and necessity in society.

In its simplest form, a data-driven process allows us to respond more effectively when making a building sensitive to its context and users. For example, in a current project at the University of Chicago, the *Campus North Residence Hall and Dining Commons*, we're designing the rooms as places for students to live and study in, not just sleep in, so comfort and performance are important. In doing so, we are using data to help us design the building's more than 800 windows. The windows have different issues – sun exposure, yes, but also operability, specific views, elevation, and even the likelihood of bird strikes. So, for instance, we're using data to design for each exposure and to fine-tune how much frit goes on each window. Being able to make value judgments based on all available criteria and real-time information allows us to simultaneously optimize a building's energy model and its habitability.

BIM input takes more time, especially when the project is unique formally, but it pays off when the information on performance helps us to make important design decisions. In general, BIM is extremely helpful once you get past that input curve. But then of course there are lots of builders not making use of information modeling. From a purely pragmatic standpoint, you can get everything coordinated among the team of design

Diagram of *Solar Carve Tower* set back along New York's *High Line* park, directing sunlight to this shared amenity (image courtesy of Studio Gang Architects)

professionals, but if the contractor doesn't use the technology, they will come up against the same conflicts that were already resolved in the BIM model. In design, we may have succeeded in "threading a needle" and were able to get a duct to fit between these two pieces of structure, but the builder won't understand that if they don't read the model, and then we have to work to adjust the duct again. There's a stumbling block there, except with more technically savvy builders. If the client requires BIM for the design team, it should be mandatory for the contractor as well.

But drawing and constructing are just the low-hanging fruit of information. Where I find the ability to use data – about the environment, the site, a material, or other phenomena – most exciting is in design research. For the studio I taught at Rice University, instead of giving the students a specific site, I required them to use data to find the best site for their project: an open-water dolphin sanctuary. They consulted available information mapping the ocean, taking into account the sometimes conflicting criteria of its use, such as drilling, shipping, and marine life. They also worked with data from the National Oceanic and Atmospheric Administration (NOAA) to understand where animals exist and thrive. Marine spatial planning is a relatively new policy development practice that hasn't employed a design approach, but it is a key area where I think architects could contribute. The studio explored this new territory, using data to locate an appropriate site specifically for the sanctuary animals that would meet their needs and accommodate other ocean uses. As designers and architects, we can bring our spatial, organizational, and strategic skills to important issues such as ocean planning to address the needs of our planet and its occupants.

Rendering of *Solar Carve Tower* shows how incident light accentuates the faceted glass wall of the solar carved surface (image courtesy of Studio Gang Architects)

Does technology (i.e., BIM broadly) help you address problems in society or is technology a bigger part of the problem than contemporary culture cares to admit?

Information access is bigger than BIM, and as with every technology, there are unintended consequences. Data provide exciting insights for designing smarter cities. But we must remain cognizant of how this information can be manipulated and what is ethical in terms of mining these data.

In construction, though, a real concern about the digital transformation is the loss of jobs and livelihoods that may result.

For workers, especially in emerging markets, jobs have disappeared and continue to disappear. Instead of fetishizing the robotically constructed building, why not continue to innovate at the low-tech end of the spectrum? Both high- and low-tech advancement will produce a healthier economy.

What are your thoughts on the afterlife (or life-cycle) of a BIM model?

I find that with institutional projects, universities are at the forefront in terms of using BIM for the facilities' afterlife. The University of Chicago, for instance, will continue to work with our model after the building is complete. It would be interesting to be able to access the university's proprietary cache of data for our post-occupancy process, to learn from the real-time data and to compare the design's performance to buildings that are nearby or similar.

Do you feel a project like the Solar Carve Tower's literal use of environmental data to determine and generate a formal response prioritizes a functional role or one of aesthetics?

It is definitely using function (slicing and carving and shaping the building) to bring light into the spaces of the site, but at the same time we evaluated the aesthetics of what the data produced. What's particularly interesting is that the shape is benefiting the public realm over the building itself. The shape is rational and functional, but we could design a million varieties of rational, functional buildings. We did in fact explore numerous iterations – of massing, façade, orientation, etc. – that all shared the basic concept and logic. But it is not necessarily always the absolute highest performing option that is chosen, because other important criteria have to be balanced. In addition to data analytics, there are more intangible aspects of form and subjectivity that are part of the process.

Does Studio Gang question the quality or necessity of information coming into design as a quantitative means of decision making? Does the simulation and analysis validate your design work to a client?

Buildings need ideas. And they need ideas on multiple levels. So I wouldn't say the response to climate is necessarily worthy of being the sole idea; there is more to architecture than that. If the overall concept is strong and, in addition to that, also integrates relevant data, then yes, it's easier to validate the work with stakeholders.

Solar Carve Tower reframes traditional zoning logic by sculpting the mass and inverts the building's setbacks along the geometric paths of the sun's rays. So you are playing with code and planning logistics of the building's area and relationship to easements and proximities.

Yes, but playing with them for the public good. In the case of Solar Carve, we found a weird exception to the site. Typically, the regulation is intended to bring light to the street. However, our street didn't need more light – it's on the west edge of Manhattan – and so our structure wouldn't significantly impact the street. The allowable as-of-right structure, though, would negatively impact the *High Line* park, blocking light and views from this public amenity. By inverting that regulation, we could set back the building from the Highline to provide more direct sunlight and views. We were able to prove this by showing a BIM model and its accompanying data.

What do you think of government and planning departments' requirement of a BIM production and submission? But more broadly, the government's involvement through BIM, like the UK requiring the use of BIM of its entire population as a solution, do you think that is too much control or involvement?

If we really want high-performing buildings and cities, we need these kinds of targets and also people in place who are checking on the targets. If there weren't requirements for government buildings to be LEED certified, it just wouldn't happen. There has to be this kind of policy and it has to be legislated through zoning. The use of green wash is prevalent, so I would be in favor of more measurement, higher goals, and tougher targets.

Has the transition from CAD to 3D software platforms opened up a literal transformation in architectural language of conventional building elements, whereby the idea of window becomes an aperture? Translation of building elements in your mind?

Solar Carve Tower rendering at night (image courtesy of Studio Gang Architects)

I've always thought about architecture three-dimensionally, but 3D software has made it easier to rationalize the complexity imagined. The software also helps to evaluate performance, which has an impact on aesthetics. If the idea of a window is tied to performance, then a window designed for a building in Denmark won't look like a window designed for a building in Brazil.

What are other natural conditions of inquiry (solar, water, wind, and natural disaster) that you have intentions to develop or investigate for the changing condition of the contemporary city?

Disaster and resiliency factors for almost every coastal city are now major issues for design. I'm hoping to do more work on improving resiliency while interweaving natural, bio-diverse environments into our cities. With our project at *Lincoln Park Zoo*, we aimed to improve resiliency with storm-water retention, create an attractive public space, and enhance biodiversity. When it was finished, many species of animals started coming back to the site due to the new landscape that had much more food value. The black-crown heron population nesting at the site increased tenfold to 400 pairs during migration. We are basically witnessing a live experiment of how closely urban and wild populations can thrive together and how we can design spaces that allow for this. Likewise, human attraction to the space multiplied, buttressed by increased programmatic uses such as education and recreation. Technology enables us to finally put value on what ecological systems are providing. Armed with this information, architects can more successfully advocate for a natural system doing the work of gray pipe infrastructure. Putting value on what nature does and can provide – that's the next big frontier for architecture.

ON PAGES 94–95
Solar Carve Tower massing studies (image courtesy of Studio Gang Architects)

5

Material practice

WHEN put in service of design output, a database and its context of information ironically seeks a contingency between the virtual and the physical world – an alliance known as material practice. Such practice generates directly from material behavior and logic and has in the last decade produced ideas and effects through the unpredictable nature of its physical artifacts.[1] Historically, digital architecture exploited a material palette primarily for its graphic representation of photorealistic rendering or animation. Such immaterial artifacts of (what was then) a new digital era led to visual demonstrations of paper-thin concrete or glass stretching with limitless elasticity. These digital explorations so challenged the practical logic of material that it caused premature skepticism of digital architecture's staying power by critics such as Aaron Betsky.[2] A returned interest in the application of real materials has coincided with the ubiquity of digital fabrication tools and led a decade of building technology to upset the discipline with its own exuberant accountability. The true advances in material information production arrive within BIM's ability to schedule, categorize, and redistribute conceptually for the physical outcome of building elements.[3]

BIM's material attributes are laden with meaning well beyond graphic appearance. Derivations from specific physical qualities, such as behavioral anisotropy, manufacturer's registration, or nominal efficiency can lead to measurable design impact and assessment. These attributes can reveal efficacies or inefficiencies long before construction begins, such that accountability of the material make-up of building elements motivates a design strategy of material parts. Generating components with their real-world attributes, often called parametric modeling, is for some designers, such as Andrew Kudless, founder of material practice MATSYS, not necessarily BIM. He claims:

> What people think of as a BIM model tends to focus on the production (i.e., building) end of things, instead of the conceptual design or generative kind of work. In the same way that a contractor

Zahner Company exterior façade material sample from the *deYoung Museum* by Herzog & deMeuron (photo credit Danelle Briscoe)

ON PAGES 98–99
BIM to parametric process diagram (image courtesy of Matt Flamm, Graduate Design Thesis, Ball State University, School of Architecture, Advisor Kevin Klinger, 2012)

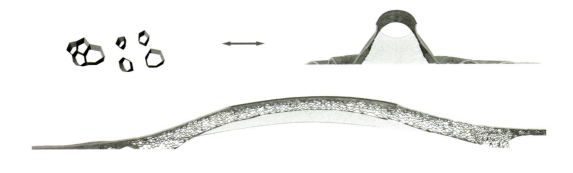

Parametric · Whole is greater than the sum of its parts

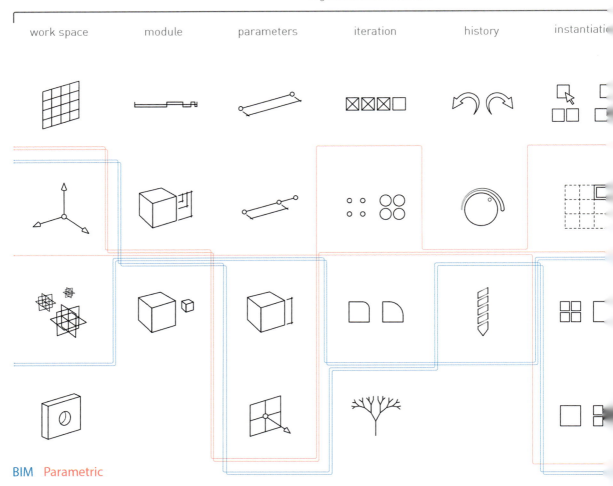

Organizational Structure

| work space | module | parameters | iteration | history | instantiation |

BIM Parametric

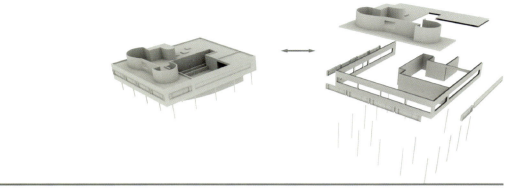

Whole is reducible to its parts • BIM

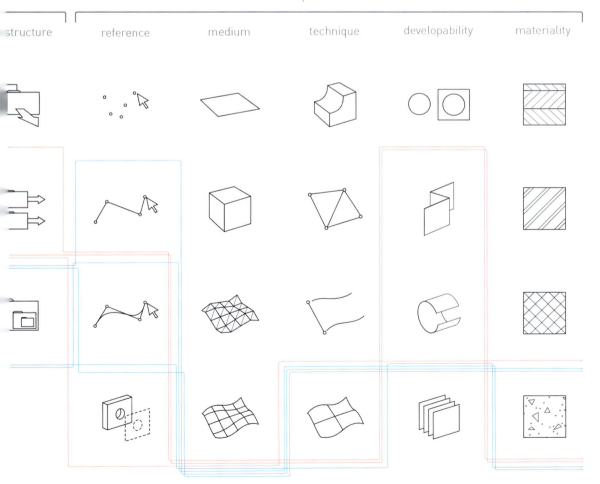

Spatial Structure

structure | reference | medium | technique | developability | materiality

does not buy a new hammer every time he needs to nail, many parts and pieces can viably (re)generate from a parametric information model for design.[4]

Alternatively, the BIM and parametric approaches have become seemingly interchangeable.[5] Incorporating material by way of system and component design, intention is no longer simply reduced to its parts, nor the sum of its whole, but includes what it means to be designing and creating with material information.

Massimal×+ (photo credit GLINTstudios, image courtesy of D.O.T.S.)

Part to whole

Both proliferation of unique parts and increased appearance of their assembly instructions defines another design aspect of material practice. In part, a suite of fabrication technologies, such as CNC milling and laser-cutting, have become standard tools to the industry and enabled this sort of studio production in general. Their abilities to effortlessly cut any shape, quantify these pieces and numerically etch their quantified parts articulate a surface with the information of its assembly. In this sense, focus on the production of material information through information etching stands equal to its ideas and effect. For most such material practitioners, the end goal is not traditional drawing documentation, but instead the direct fabrication of full-scale, physical and custom pieces that literally wear the numerical values from their 3D model file.[6]

As practitioners occupied with material exploration, the concept of BIM allows Akari Takebayashi and Jason Scroggin, co-Principals of Design Office Takebayashi Scroggin (D.O.T.S.), to set up rules to focus their process. Their belief is that BIM cannot override other aspects of design:

> There is a danger in prioritizing the technical capabilities of a project too early on in the design process. Technology is one aspect of our methodology – a process that tends to lie in a hybrid condition between material logic and empirical evidence through manual testing, craft, and intuition.[7]

Digital techniques at full scale and attention to the inherent material system of parts and pieces define their unique, animal-like characters.

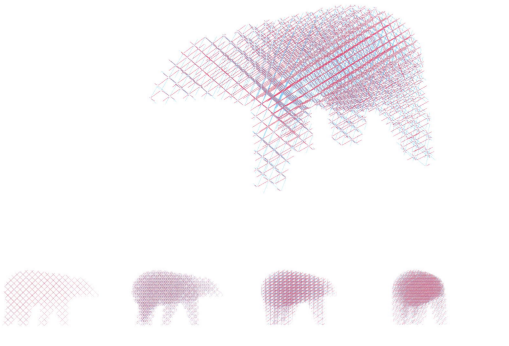

Their *Massimal* series are playful visceral masses, each manufactured out of a single material. To schedule all the parts to each mass, D.O.T.S. use a model for reference and, depending on whether the component is fixed or flexible, lay out each assembly piece virtually. They then develop the material system in relation to the size of the object to determine the final resolution of the figure without losing the affinity of the animal shape and actual material stability.

The latest 2014 iteration, *Massimal*×+, is a volumetric space frame assembled from a kit of parts. The pre-fabricated construct is made up of only two unique types of element: one stock rod material and the other 3D printed custom connectors. It contains fixed connections with the component size and placement precisely determined. The hybrid material condition shifts between digital procedures and physical material constructs to afford scalable research. D.O.T.S. input the material thicknesses to determine the resolution, and often the color, for reference and aesthetic purposes. When a material system is surface-oriented rather than volumetric, the resolution (or number of parts) is set to the moment where the form remains a smooth geometry, producing as few contiguous templates as possible. As a way to quantify for off-site assembly, every piece is modeled. D.O.T.S. strives to have their building projects inspire the interaction and playfulness that motivates their current material productions.

Material analysis of the *Oslo International School* (project credit Jarmund/Vigsnæs AS Architects, photo credit Ivan Brodey, graphic courtesy of Hannah Zhang, University of Texas at Austin School of Architecture, Advanced Studio taught by Assistant Professor Danelle Briscoe, 2010)

Material take-off

A component and system approach defines a building element in both macro and micro conditions. Factors of material – characteristics, volume, as well as the full assessment of its aligning parts – develop a material strategy that is increasingly abstracting material category or quantity with color. In this sense, material representation becomes simplified by its conception, while the information content it holds has expanded tenfold. Having this analytical capacity of developing the embedded information content, architects have a new approach to the traditional design research of case study precedents.

Analyzing a built project's systems and components often leads to a pared-down diagram that – at best – shows the organization of the building's functional layout, structure, or circulation. In BIM, precedent research can further disassemble the components and their material strategy, thereby transforming an analytical model into a generative or

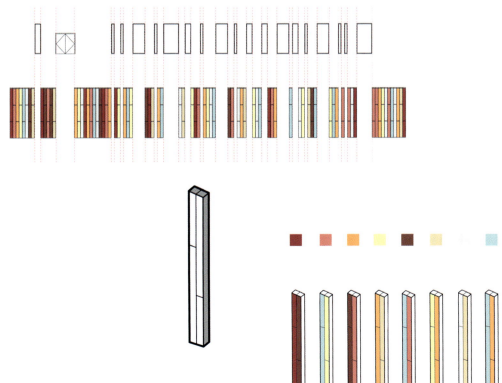

live diagram. In attempting to understand BIM as a design tool, academic research analyzes the material consequences of precedent, such as the *Oslo International School* refurbishment in Bekkestua, Norway. This example takes the original material motives of project architects, Jarmund/Vigsnæs AS, and transforms the design approach through model research.[8] The case study's brightly colored vertical metal panels elevate the design of a fairly straightforward, rectilinear façade. By reducing the facade to its window types and stripe panel strategy, a student can then take authorship over these parametric material and building elements in a way that allows for adaptation to alternative site, program, or application relationships. In this design exercise, alternative criteria, such as a different color pattern variation, can be activated through the precedent's BIM framework. The metal building panel element can vary according to development of the material type, quantity, color, and placement along the wall. Such conceptual re-use – a method often shunned in some design circles – results in the flexibility of visual character, amplification of variation for a standard wall, and design exploration through precedent analysis. Outputs, including material take-off schedules and delivery sequences, can no longer be solely reputed as mundane when their visual display can easily be engaged as a design document.

Such design documents additionally serve as the necessary abstraction to quantify the material, organize variation of building elements, and map out configurations on-site for a project. In 2013, Governor Andrew M. Cuomo of New York presented a dramatic transformation to the City of Buffalo's largely vacant outer harbor. The *Canal Side* portion of 350 acres of waterfront by the Erie Harbor Development was dedicated to rest and recreation projects with proposals of several granite bridges. In an effort to camouflage these insertions, each piece of stone for each bridge was designed with a unique length and height. To achieve and coordinate this material variation, the Pike Company, one of the largest design-build companies in the northeast United States, used high-definition laser scanning and BIM to locate and nestle these stone pieces tightly into the landscape. This contextual information applied to each bridge was then used to inform and randomize the pattern of the cut granite layout. Pike Company's BIM model colorized and parameterized each unique piece of granite for layout, procurement, and basic physical constraints: foundation location, cap stone determinant, and the limits of each wall's start and finish. Eighth inch tolerances suggest a greater degree of

Canal Side BIM (image courtesy of the Erie Harbor Development, Pike Construction)

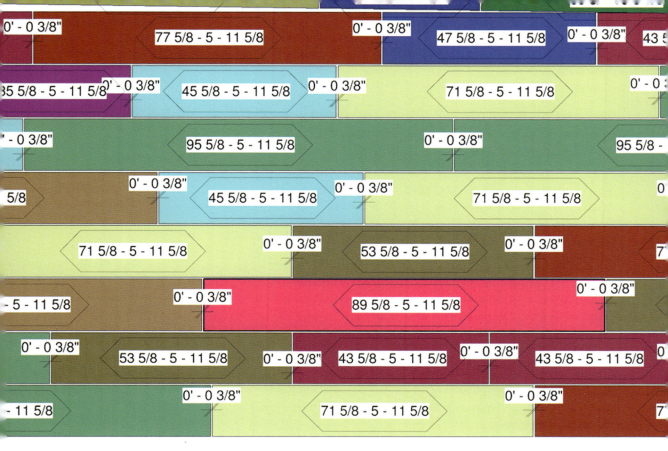

confidence in the control afforded by BIM. The stone coursing adhered to two parametric rules: a limitation on the number of similar length pieces, and the proximity range of those similar lengths. The BIM parametric process ensured that no overlap was less than 11 inches and that this basic construction procedure was efficient and effective for the many stakeholders involved in a government project of this scale.

Designers can now also leverage BIM to measure the embodied environmental footprints of design variations. KT Innovations (KTI), an affiliate of the award-winning architecture firm Kieran Timberlake, created a BIM plug-in to provide users with critical building materials information. Within the same time frame, pace, and environment of the design process, this BIM plug-in, known as *Tally*, takes the usable floor space of a building under study and calculates the amount of material required to produce the given design goals.

Tally also combines material attributes, for example the potential global warming comparative values of using, say, corrugated shingles instead of metal panels. A manufacturer's assembly details and material take-off quantifications are also scheduled with each design option. And further, the architectural specifications coincide with environmental impact data.

The real-time life cycle assessment (LCA) adds a critical layer of information for whole-building analysis through its material nature, including comparative results of iterative design options.[9] From raw material extraction through processing, manufacturing, distribution, use, repair, and maintenance, and disposal or recycling, this parallel LCA process can help a BIM material practice avoid a narrow outlook on environmental concerns.[10] For the University of Texas at Austin 2015 Solar Decathlon submission, *NexasHaus*, the goal of their *Tally LCA* was to determine what construction material (structural material, insulation material, etc.) and what system (standard stick framing, advanced framing, or cross laminated timber (CLT)) had the least amount of environmental impact. According to the *Tally LCA* cradle-to-grave analysis, advanced stick frame construction for the same thermal performance in the building envelope proved to have the least overall environmental impact and thus have elected to build with this system to optimize their construction method. In addition, the lightweight system of stick framing outperformed the heavyweight CLT in manufacturing and end-of-life stages.

An additional step was taken from the *Tally* results to convert the *NexasHaus* environmental "savings" calculated from kilograms of CO_2

NexasHaus Life Cycle Analysis (image courtesy of KT Innovations and University of Texas at Austin School of Architecture, Solar Decathalon Team 2014–2015)

Results per Revit Category, itemized by Material

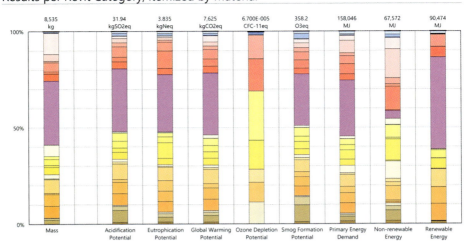

	Mass	Acidification Potential	Eutrophication Potential	Global Warming Potential	Ozone Depletion Potential	Smog Formation Potential	Primary Energy Demand	Non-renewable Energy	Renewable Energy
	8,535 kg	31.94 kgSO2eq	3.835 kgNeq	7,625 kgCO2eq	6.700E-05 CFC-11eq	358.2 O3eq	158,046 MJ	67,572 MJ	90,474 MJ

Legend

Doors
- Door frame, wood, no door
- Glazing, double, 6mm, laminated safety glass
- Glazing, double, insulated (argon), low-E
- Stainless steel, door hardware, lever lock, exterior, residential

Floors
- Domestic hardwood, US
- Domestic softwood, US
- Expanded polystyrene (EPS), board
- Exterior grade plywood, US
- Fiberglass blanket insulation, unfaced
- None
- Self-adhering, polymer-modified asphalt sheet underlayment

Roofs
- Domestic softwood, US
- Expanded polystyrene (EPS), board
- Exterior grade plywood, US
- Fiberglass blanket insulation, unfaced
- None
- TPO roofing membrane, sheet, white
- Wall board, gypsum, natural

Windows
- Galvanized steel tilt-turn window fittings for wood- and PVC
- Glazing, double, insulated (argon), low-E
- Window frame, wood, operable

Structure
- Domestic hardwood, US
- None

Walls
- Domestic softwood, US
- Expanded polystyrene (EPS), board
- Exterior grade plywood, US
- Fiberglass blanket insulation, unfaced
- None
- Self-adhering, polymer-modified asphalt sheet underlayment
- Wall board, gypsum, natural

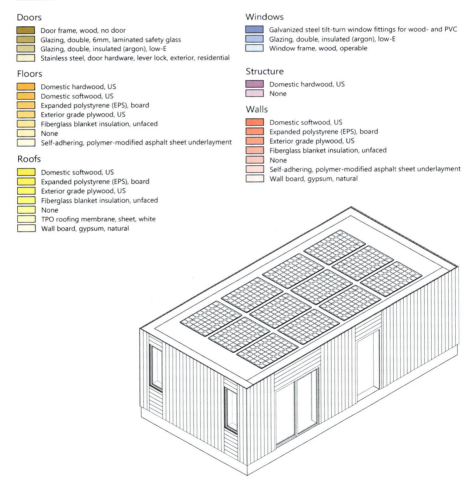

equivalent to things like gallons of gasoline so that the average person can recognize the magnitude of the results once the project is on display. During the tour, the *Nexushaus* will have QR codes throughout the building, embedding information on the materials used in the design process. When scanned, images like the *Tally LCA* will display on a visitor's phone or tablet to explain why choices were made for the specific material/construction method.[11]

Diagram of embedded material BIM data (image courtesy of Morphosis Architects)

Material workflow

In 1929, Walter Gropius made the call for a high-rise city of light, air, and mobility. Global development continues to frame Gropius' rules of function and materiality through formal responses that now also includes data, information, and knowledge.[12] Morphosis, a renowned Los Angeles-based architecture firm, demonstrates material information of component parts as a driver in the configuration of their work. For the *Tour Phare*, a tower soon to be the tallest new building in France since the Eiffel Tower, Morphosis created a non-standard form with varying glass panels expressing the movement of changing light – becoming opaque, translucent, or transparent from different sun angles and vantage points.

Thom Mayne, the Design Director that founded Morphosis in 1972, believes a building's form is the result of a variety of forces ranging from program to aesthetics. The *Tour Phare* adheres to this principle, but focuses more specifically on influencing material factors to shape its exterior envelope. With the expectation of producing a cultural landmark, the scale and the complexity of the building systems (i.e., façades, atrium, pavilion, etc.) becomes necessary to meet this ethereal design intention. The design team established custom database tools for material development, integration of performance metrics, and geometric rationalization. According to Cory Bruegger, Morphosis' Director of Design Technology, the project required a combination of physical prototyping, parametric modeling, computational design, and some custom plug-ins for the optimization of the final material construct.[13] Specifics ranging from dynamic relaxation analysis for the structural dia-grid to widgets for the instantiation of detailed façade components provided the team with the means to understand the complexity of the project. The team was subsequently able to extract the performance metrics of each iteration, and to identify the unique conditions of the building material assemblies.[14]

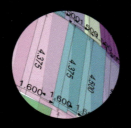
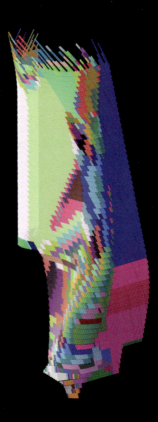

- 1046 panels (1.20x4.60m)
- 707 panels (1.30x4.60m)
- 656 panels (1.40x4.10m)
- 381 panels (1.40x4.00m)
- 146 panels (1.40x3.90m)
- 112 panels (1.50x4.60m)
- 111 panels (1.40x4.60m)
- 91 panels (1.40x4.70m)
- 91 panels (1.20x4.50m)
- 72 panels (1.30x4.80m)
- 71 panels (1.30x4.70m)
- 69 panels (1.30x4.40m)
- 64 panels (1.50x4.00m)
- 61 panels (1.40x4.50m)
- 55 panels (1.50x4.10m)
- 51 panels (1.20x4.70m)
- 46 panels (1.30x4.30m)
- 46 panels (1.20x4.40m)
- 46 panels (1.40x4.80m)
- 44 panels (1.50x4.20m)
- 44 panels (1.30x4.20m)
- 41 panels (1.30x4.90m)
- 40 panels (1.50x4.50m)
- 40 panels (1.30x4.50m)
- 39 panels (1.60x4.40m)
- 39 panels (1.20x4.80m)
- 39 panels (1.40x4.20m)
- 36 panels (1.50x4.30m)
- 34 panels (1.20x6.90m)
- 33 panels (1.30x3.90m)
- 33 panels (1.50x3.90m)
- 33 panels (1.20x4.10m)
- 31 panels (1.40x4.40m)
- 31 panels (1.30x4.10m)
- 31 panels (1.60x4.50m)
- 30 panels (1.50x4.40m)
- 27 panels (1.30x4.00m)
- 27 panels (1.40x4.90m)
- 27 panels (1.30x5.00m)
- 27 panels (1.40x4.30m)
- 24 panels (1.20x4.90m)
- 23 panels (1.20x4.00m)
- 22 panels (1.20x5.10m)
- 22 panels (1.60x4.00m)
- 21 panels (1.30x3.80m)
- 21 panels (1.20x4.20m)
- 18 panels (1.40x7.30m)
- 18 panels (1.20x5.00m)
- 17 panels (1.30x5.10m)
- 15 panels (1.50x5.00m)
- 15 panels (1.60x4.30m)
- 14 panels (1.40x2.80m)
- 14 panels (1.60x4.10m)
- 14 panels (1.60x4.20m)
- 13 panels (1.50x4.70m)
- 12 panels (1.60x3.90m)
- 12 panels (1.20x7.30m)
- 11 panels (1.60x4.60m)
- 10 panels (1.20x5.20m)
- 10 panels (1.50x4.80m)
- 10 panels (1.70x4.10m)
- 9 panels (1.10x3.80m)
- 9 panels (1.30x5.20m)
- 9 panels (1.50x4.90m)
- 7 panels (1.30x3.70m)
- 6 panels (1.20x3.90m)
- 6 panels (1.50x5.10m)
- 5 panels (1.70x4.20m)
- 5 panels (1.40x5.00m)
- 5 panels (1.70x4.50m)
- 5 panels (1.20x5.30m)
- 4 panels (1.10x4.80m)
- 4 panels (1.20x4.30m)
- 4 panels (1.40x5.10m)
- 3 panels (1.70x4.60m)
- 3 panels (1.60x4.90m)
- 3 panels (1.50x5.20m)
- 3 panels (1.70x4.70m)
- 3 panels (1.20x3.80m)
- 3 panels (1.30x7.30m)
- 3 panels (1.70x4.40m)
- 2 panels (1.40x3.70m)
- 2 panels (1.00x4.30m)
- 2 panels (1.20x3.00m)
- 2 panels (1.20x5.40m)
- 2 panels (1.30x5.30m)
- 2 panels (1.10x3.90m)
- 2 panels (1.60x5.00m)
- 2 panels (1.20x1.50m)
- 2 panels (1.60x4.80m)
- 2 panels (1.60x4.70m)
- 26 unique panels
- total 5129 panels

The "double-skin" façade system, in particular, demonstrates the primary roles of the project's materiality of information. The two skins are placed so that air flows in the intermediate cavity, minimizing heat gain and glare, and allowing sufficient daylighting for the interior spaces. Additionally, the high-performance skin transforms the shape of the building with changes in light throughout the day – becoming opaque, translucent, or transparent from different vantage points. Critical diagrams used in the design process demonstrate the types of information visualizations used for material considerations of the double-skin panels. The data and color coding are extracted from the design model to assess and evaluate design options. As a prerequisite for assessing each panel's overall performance, the orientation of the panel relative to the solar path is noted, with an indication of the date and time where it is most effective. Furthermore, data from horizontal and vertical angles of panels relative to the curtain wall of the building establish the depth of the exterior catwalks to ensure access for maintenance and safety. Each color defines an angle range for quick visualization of the results. Panel dimensions and rationalization of the panels into building element groupings anticipate that each color indicates a single panel type, both documented and quantified.

As is the case with other Morphosis projects, the *Tour Phare* project generated several BIM innovations to meet the scale and complexity of the building's material systems. Fluid dynamic (CFD) and wind tunnel analysis assessed the impact of wind on the tower, site, and surrounding buildings for each custom panel. The combined impact of energy production and natural ventilation systems on the building's electrical and mechanical efficiency provided a framework to assess lifecycle costs and client return on investment. With an expected completion in 2016, the project remains to be seen.

One current by-product for the firm is a highly developed and detailed BIM library of components for glazing systems, exterior screens, and metal enclosures. These prototypical components automatically update with essential project data – information that can range from overall panel geometry (length, width, panel area, and geometric control points) to performance data like material composition, solar heat gain coefficient, and visible light transmission. This workflow theoretically implies a viable upstream consideration of material optimization of the built outcome.

Tour Phare rendering (courtesy of Morphosis Architects)

BIM outcome

For many in practice, materiality separates a building fantasy from its reality. The *Kilden Performing Arts Centre*, designed by ALA Architects in 2011, is a prime example of a project's monumental use of material as threshold, where the audience moves from a natural physical setting in Kristiansand, Norway to the realm of performance within the theatre space. The undulating ceiling/wall, made of solid local oak planks, is not only a disguised theatrical effect, but a tactile artifact that acoustically improves the foyer. The infinite blackness of the other façades emphasizes the spectacle of the wood feature at the scale of the building.

ALA Architects completed the project according to the original competition design, and within the given time frame and budget. This is no small task considering the 4,000 m^2 oak surface contains 14,309 unique glue-laminated girders and twisted oak boards. According to the project's lead designer, Juho Grönholm, "Although the client did not require it, the whole design group was at all instances using BIM."[15] Accordingly, consultants for the mechanical, acoustical, structural, and other systems coordinated work with the help of the 3D database model, especially for material quantities and calculations. Grönholm reflects on a contractor who chose not to use the BIM model and was quite fixed on using traditional paper prints. As the construction progressed, the oppositional contractor became interested in the BIM approach, so much so that he began incorporating BIM coordination and model checker tools himself. Designers in this instance are redefining the building culture through construction, not the other way around, where the construction industry determines the direction of practice.

Significantly, the BIM to CNC process made it possible to fabricate all the individual components at almost the same cost of mass production. The sub-contractor, in close cooperation with timber specialists, relied on Design to Production (DP) to model and develop a pre-fabrication and assembly strategy through a parametric model. Grönholm claims that while the price for machining stays the same, the effort for planning and logistics rose with the number of different parts. And when it came to the thousands, every second lost for an additional part added up to man-hours of work on the project. In response, DP set up digital production chains from the design right to the machine, automating plan generation and fabrication data, and ensuring both quality and flexibility at the same time. The project demonstrates the

Kilden Performing Arts Centre BIM model (image courtesy of Hanno Stehling at designtoproduction)

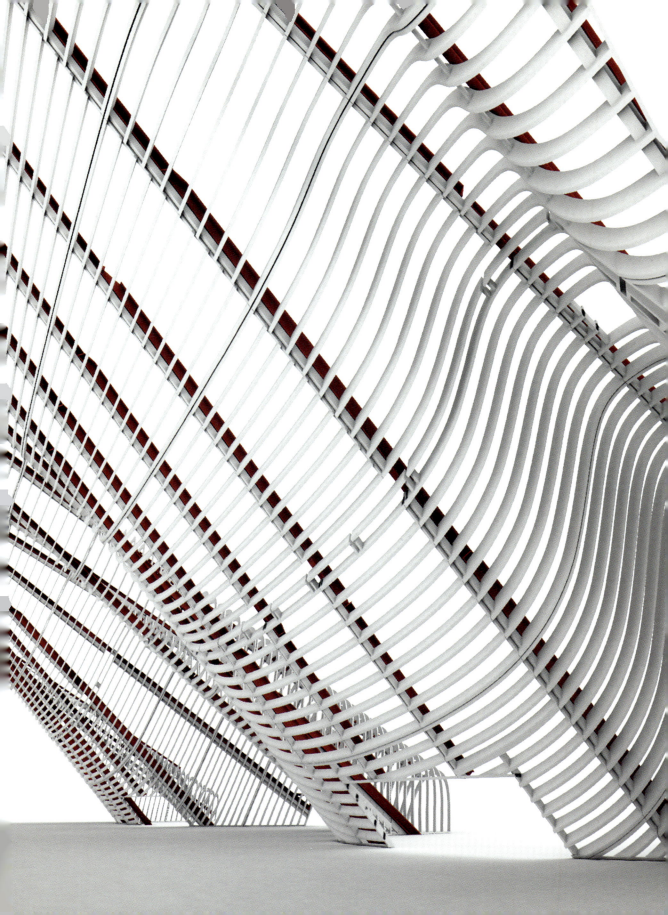

necessity of using BIM at this scale – and in cooperation with fabrication experts – to manufacture components for complex structures with computer-controlled tools.

Conclusion

Modes of material visualization, distribution, and networking have the capacity to be key factors in a design vocabulary. Color abstraction as material code becomes a playful measure incorporating more information about a material, but requires a new kind of training to "read" color as data, and data as material, in design. Ultimately, this attention to material categorization counters the heritage of 3D representations. Moreover, it critically shifts information acquisition to the material workflow.

Admittedly, those designers whose work values information that is not quite a building *yet* sometimes view the BIM data-driven approach as a limitation rather than an advantage. BIM's advantage of better integrating architecture with the building industry by standardizing building components will soon coincide with parametric modeling, which is better known to enable design of unique and geometrically challenging component systems, whose intentions are consistently found to be in service of and scalable to the act of building. BIM holds more facts about a material's building application, but sometimes those facts may limit the opportunity to push a material beyond its known conditions. Modes of working to understand the complex relationship between the part and the whole are currently tied more to a design mindset and less to specific digital modeling tools. Data quality is judged by its precision, be it measured, calculated, or estimated. The completeness and uniformity of the methodology applied on a study serving as a data source also give depth and meaning. Not unlike the uncertainty in the realm of design indecision, ambiguity now stems from both materialized data and its application.

Notes
1. Robert McAnulty, "What's the Matter with Material?" *LOG* 5 (New York, NY: Anyone Corporation, 2005), pp. 87–92.
2. Aaron Betsky, "A Virtual Reality," *Artforum* (September 2007): 441–449.
3. ArchiCAD offers a gravity function to automatically place the new element directly on top of a slab, roof, shell, or mesh on the same story, thus taking on the elevation of the element it is placed on.
4. Andrew Kudless, interview with the author, February 21, 2014.

5   Matt Flamm, *Digital Modeling Tools: Sculpting Project Organization*. Ball State University, School of Architecture, Graduate Design Thesis, Advisor Kevin Klinger, 2012, pp. 8–19.
6   Claim made by three interviewees: Andrew Kudless, Elena Manferdini, and Marc Fornes.
7   Akari Takebayashi and Jason Scroggin, interview with the author, September 30, 2014.
8   Rene Chang spoke to the importance of the pedagogical structure with which to introduce BIM (Autodesk Yale University BIM Symposium, New Haven, CT, April 10, 2010). Her thoughts influenced the Advanced Studio offering in 2010 at the University of Texas at Austin School of Architecture. Diagram created by Master candidate, Hannah Zhang.
9   Roderick Bates, Tally Director, email to the author, July 30, 2014. Some information deduced from "Tally LCA App for Autodesk Revit," *kierantimberlake.com*, http://kierantimberlake.com/pages/view/95/tally/parent (retrieved September 2, 2014).
10 "Life Cycle Assessment," *United States Environmental Protection Agency*, www.epa.gov/nrmrl/std/lca/lca.html (retrieved October 14, 2014).
11 Julia Park, University of Texas at Austin Architecture/Architectural Engineering Honors Program student, email exchange with the author, December 18, 2014.
12 Walter Gropius, "Die Wohnformen: Flach-, Mittel- oder Hochbau?," *Das Neue Berlin* (1929): 93.
13 Cory Bruegger, email interview with the author, July 29, 2014.
14 Database formats included dgn (Bentley), dwg (Autodesk), CATPart/Pdrouct (Dassault), and IFC.
15 Kilden's lead designer, Juho Grönholm, email exchange with the author, September 3, 2014.

Bibliography

Cheng, R. (2006). Questioning the Role of BIM in Architectural Education. University of Minnesota. www.aecbytes.com/viewpoint/2006/issue_26.html (retrieved March 2011).

Klinger, K. and Kolarevic, B. *Manufacturing Material Effects: Rethinking Design and Making in Architecture*. New York, NY: Routledge, 2008.

[INTERVIEW]

Julie Eizenberg
KONING EIZENBERG ARCHITECTURE

Does Koning Eizenberg Architecture regard material information or data as essential to thinking about design?

Let's start with materials. For us, materials are one aspect, but not the essential aspect, to thinking about design. Materials are chosen as often for their familiarity (so we know how they perform) as their novelty. The *Sobieski Pool House* is a good example. Cellular polycarbonate is not a new material and was one of a range of transparent options. The sensibility of the material is the information we seek and we work from that to highlight its contribution to the whole. We do like doing things as cheaply as possible. These days this might just as likely mean leveraging a traditional fabrication process, like metal punching, as was the case at the *28th St Apartments*, as a digital fabrication process was needed to achieve the fluid shaped wood ceiling at *Temple Israel*.

And by data I assume you mean a BIM model. Clearly if we are counting on digital fabrication we are counting on a BIM model. It is essential for various fabrication options and it is increasingly more essential to our design methodology on a number of levels *but* we see it as a means to an end not a generator of design.

Would you consider your practice a material practice?

No – that is if a material practice is one whose generative process emerges from the potential of the material. I did get a chance to think that way a few years ago. The International Masonry Institute held an exhibition they called *Masonry Variations*, at the National Building Museum in Washington, DC and we were invited, among others like Jeanne Gang and Winka Dubbledam, to pair with a masonry craftsperson to investigate new possibilities for a particular masonry material category. They wanted us to imagine new ways of doing things that would help their constituency see where the future of

Pico Branch Library entrance
(photo credit Eric Staudenmaier Photography)

masonry trades might go. I investigated terrazzo and started to realize how the categorization of materials has completely changed. Terrazzo no longer generally has a cement matrix, but instead uses a synthetic resin. So even though it is still considered a masonry trade, it actually has nothing much to do with masonry any more. It may have pebbles embedded in it, but really that's it. If you make wallpaper and you put an image of a rock on it, is it masonry? The way we categorize materials and label trades is becoming more of a needed political construct to protect labor interests – which makes perfect sense.

More usually we work from an idea and then think "what material or assembly is best suited for it within the budget we have?" Our practice is strategic at its core and certainly interested in materials and fabrication possibilities, but it is all in service to the big idea. It is not the generator.

Does BIM make detailing your specific material palettes more difficult or play a critical role in achieving this phase of a project?

It depends on the trade. For the *Pico Branch Library* in Santa Monica we designed a folded roof and steel arbor that required digital fabrication. The steel industry has transformed very quickly and the fabrication details ran smoothly. We did run into an issue with the library screens that have a shadow pattern effect that needed to be water-jet cut using a digital file. The contract for that work went to an old-fashioned metal siding shop. The old-fashioned siding shop finally located the right person to cut the panels, but had none of the right resources to provide the fabricator with digital field-measured files. So they wanted us to provide field-measured files. We did not want to get caught between the general contractor and the sub but for that project delivery framework (design, bid, build) it was the only way to achieve the design intent. If someone in the construction loop doesn't have the skill set for the expected technology, getting it done can really get sticky. Construction is a very big industry with a lot of inertia and a lot of unskilled labor and this example – I am sure – is not uncommon.

Is there modularity to the way you design?

I wish there was. That is actually where the BIM thing can be so silly. You can get a dimension in the model that is 4'3^{11}/$_{16}$" or some crazy odd number. Really? You can't leave that on the drawings. It is a fallacy that a building can be built as precisely as we can draw it. The traditional (non-BIM) drafting practice was predicated on the assumption of drawing the minimum needed to control the outcome. There was always that hanging dimension that you were willing to flex. Because BIM measures everything the assumption on buildable tolerances is just misleading for conventional construction. One can't expect budget-built stick construction to be perfectly true or dimensionally close – tolerances run inches rather than four decimal points. BIM can mislead us to think we can be more precise than we really can.

Do you speculate on a future BIM or, put another way, do you have a BIM wish-list?

I equate BIM with Revit, which is incorrect I know – Revit is a BIM visualization/database for design but not the only tool available for design as much as many believe it is. So what do I wish for? I wish for a smoother integration of different modes of visualization into a growing BIM model. Revit requires too much precise information to initiate design ideas and the quality of the visualization appears too fixed. I do miss the clear cut-off points of twentieth-century documentation. Traditionally, for example, you would do your schematic set and in changing to your DD set, you would revisit (and, yes, draw) everything again. What happens more naturally with Revit is that visualization just evolves without clear articulation of what idea is a placeholder and what thought through. We have instituted more in-depth internal design reviews at each phase to catch as much as we can but I would love an integrated check system as well. Maybe each phase of documents could be color-coded, requiring the team to address all items to change color prior to completion of the next phase. And yes, you can track who drew what, and when, through management software but that is TMI (too much information): I crave an embedded, simpler, more intuitive mechanism.

ON PAGES 120–121
Pico Branch Library roof and panel detailing (photo credit Eric Staudenmaier Photography)

To what extent to you see a BIM extending beyond the life of its outcome? Are you currently incorporating BIM facilities maintenance on any projects through post-occupancy?

Pico Branch Library interior (photo credit Eric Staudenmaier Photography)

Not doing anything post-occupancy yet, but I think it is the way to go. There are interesting add-ons to the BIM context that are changing how we do construction observation. The construction manager I was working with on the *Belmar Apartments* had his iPad loaded with something called BlueBuild. It contains the BIM file for the project and it has the capability to sync and locate any photograph he takes in a room to the BIM through GPS. So there is a whole different expectation of how you go about doing construction observation and what the BIM means at that phase.

At the same time, every time a new technology, or aspect thereof, gives us more information about the world, the expectation of what the architect needs to provide to give instruction escalates. It is not enough to say "Move the HVAC above that." You actually have to mark it on a 3D photograph for them to feel they have enough information. So the amount of time we spend assuring people that they have all the information they need keeps expanding with the tools that allow us to harness the potential of the BIM armature.

For the *Thinkery*, the new Austin Children's Museum, were real material values used as a primary resource to develop a generative process in BIM?

Well, if you want to talk about the *Thinkery*, the issue was the metal. The kinds of details you need to make a building look abstract are not the cheapest or the most common. In order to diminish the apparent thickness of the metal panel, we basically wanted every corner joint to appear to be a butt joint and not a wrapped corner. This is not so easy to achieve when the metal is used as the waterproofing skin. In essence we were trying to simulate a rain screen, a much more expensive assembly that doesn't rely on the metal to provide a weather-tight assembly, in order to save money. This simulation was tricky for two reasons: the need to account for necessary flashing and sealing as well as the conventional expectations of how metal siding is traditionally detailed. The truth is, contractors do not always look at the drawings, especially the details. In budget construction, sub-contractors often assume what they are supposed to do based on conventional practice. Yes, we are meant to get detailed shop drawings and mockups but we often get neither. There are many intersections between architectural expression and conventional practice which are not in sync, as was

Thinkery Museum entrance
(photo credit Whit Preston)

the case here. We did eventually work through details using a mock-up, but the sub was initially a little put-out and surprised in spite of what was in the documents. If you have the owner and time on your side, conventional construction can be tweaked – if not it is difficult. It is an interesting game.

So was BIM an enabler or inhibitor for the *Thinkery*?

I think there is a belief that because a team uses a 3D tool like BIM that there will be no flaws in the system. After our design phase was complete, there were discrepancies in the drawings, like a detail not matching the section. Some junior team members responded that that was impossible: "We did it all in BIM." Actually we didn't. Details are keyed but generally for projects like this, not all components are built three-dimensionally in the model – it takes too long and doesn't necessarily facilitate the outcome. People understand the potential and intent of BIM but don't understand it is a framework – it is up to the design team to flush out the integrated content in a cost-effective manner relative to the project in hand.

In many cases BIM is just thinly disguising a 2D sensibility and wallpapering conventionalized design approaches – frankly Revit default settings all encourage such practice. It is fair to tell a client you are using BIM if you are, but for some offices it really is just a marketing ploy that "suggests" innovation and efficiency. What is actually being sold is expedience. Those architects may achieve some efficiencies that provide for a cheaper service but they are not pursuing higher-quality outcomes.

What other conditions of data inquiry or collaboration (beyond structural and mechanical engineers) does Koning Eizenberg Architecture intend to develop for a specific project or your design process in general?

Our design process remains collaborative with an increasingly more direct interaction with trades and fabricators, and I am sure that evolving construction methodology will change the way we use the BIM model. We also continue to be invested in user-based design and hope to get a better handle on metrics to validate (or not) the value of design for community spaces.

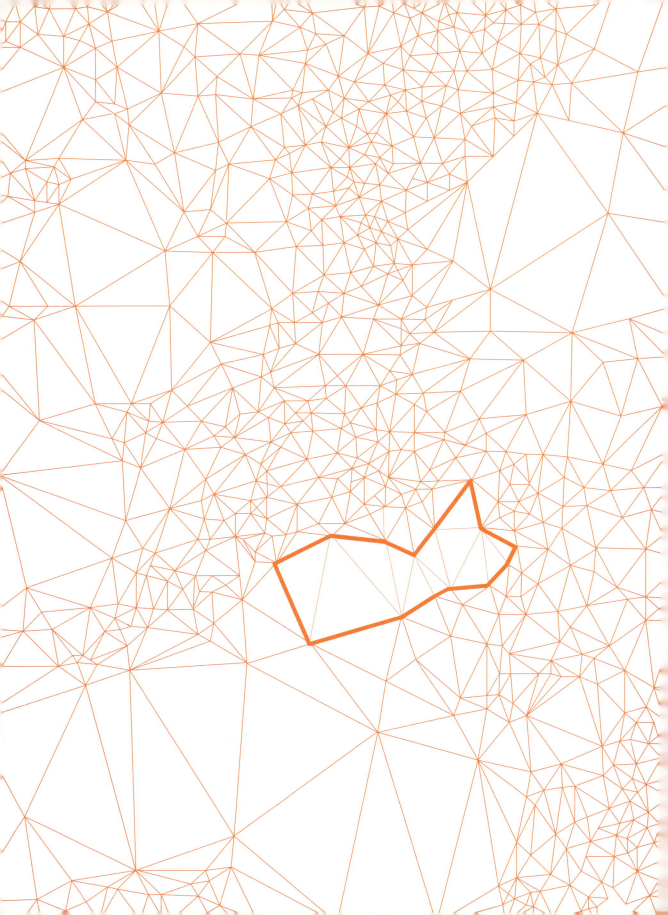

6
Geomimicry

In rethinking the agency of design, architecture increasingly draws from ideas, practices, and techniques of the sciences. Looking to geology and geography, for example, designers apply BIM data in ways that support the reconsideration of a building's conventional relationship to the earth's surfaces. To this end, potent expression and visualization of form rests staunchly on, in, or like the surrounding it mimics. The increased use of techniques for shape-blending, structural dynamics, and parametric definition arose in part from the issues investigated by Bernard Cache's *Earth Moves* in the mid-1990s. Having close to two decades to contemplate the logic and fluid connectivity of discrete building elements, this next generation of formalism positions itself as one of constructability, which then affects the consideration of surfaces, especially those that form the intersection between built-form and land-form. "A field of surfaces thus governs the object that has now become the set of possibilities of their intersection," Cache wrote in 1995, "But the surface of the object also becomes separated from its function when the latter is no longer mechanical or electronic."[1] Cache made a clear distinction between the object and the surfaces that compose it, and he claimed that the phenomenon of surface morphology becomes disconnected from the object's function while it is in the process of mutating. More specifically, the methods of mutation by which architects define a boundary between figure and ground now derive from the capabilities of the information model.[2]

Often inaccurately conflated or used interchangeably, geological and geographical data inform a building's surface function in different ways. A building may formally look or behave like a rock outcropping, or instead embed strategies of Earth's characteristics in its components. Together, a geomimetic approach ties concepts to the earth, produces difference on the earth, and articulates an earthen subjectivity – referring to the visual image that structures its physical presence. Neither as subjectively tailored or obsessively empirical, geomimetic characteristics offer rich themes for architectural abstraction.[3]

Triangulated Irregular Network
(image courtesy of Danelle Briscoe)

Geo-visualization

Eduard Imhof's distinguished text, *Cartographic Relief Presentation*, framed cartography in 1965 as an unusual synergy of technology and art. His research expanded upon the accuracy and density of survey points generated by the positional technology methods of seventeenth-century mapping, but then emphasized the representational dimensionality of Earth's crevices and peaks more artistically. Such graphic manipulation demonstrates geologic features, such as a mountain range, as inhabitable form and space through shadow and highlighted edges. Many other mid-twentieth-century design projects, such as Buckminster Fuller's *Dymaxion* projection, obsessed with representation of the Earth and its reconfigured surface as a design concept, conflating the accuracy and density of survey points of the world into a single cartographic system of geometry. Each triangular edge of the *Dymaxion* matches the scale of a partial great circle on a corresponding globe. Points within each facet shrink toward its middle, rather than enlarging to the peripheries.[4] Fuller's method critiques "traditional world maps that merely reinforce the separation of humanity," offering a premonition to the dominance of patterns and emerging relationships from the ever-evolving and accelerating process of globalization due to information connectivity.[5]

More recently, Vicente Guallart, designer and author of *Geologics: Geography Information Architecture*, cites geometry as a test bed for self-similar and multi-scalar natural elements found in geological matter. For the *Fugee Port Competition Project* in Taiwan, Guallart engaged graphic triangulation to translate the structural patterns of the fishing port's particular geographic meaning and relationship to the sea. For example, the detailed data collection of the supporting porous volcanic rock bed transforms into individualized steep roofs for the project. The graphic pattern of the rock processes a fictitious nature of contouring and geometric relationships as suggested by Imhof. This results in a practice that is one step closer to the natural artifice than the disassociated mapping challenged by Fuller's "island of humanity" projection. The precision of available data sits in sharp contrast to the abstraction of a Cartesian system; offering architects new opportunities to interpret contour in architectural form within BIM. The use of geospatial data, combined with design decision-making, upholds "site" unconventionally and makes available a literal transformation of architectural language. A roof, for example, now blurs into a fifth elevation with hyper-awareness of the rooftop surface, or terrain, and the influential surroundings it responds to.

Three-dimensional, oblique hill shading (image courtesy of Eduard Imhof, *Cartographic Relief Presentation*, De Gruyter 1982, illustration p. 184, fig 132: Todi Group – Klausen Passen – Pragel Pass)

In the simplest terms, surface context appropriates geographic information system (GIS) data sets to assist in the visualization of geological representation. The aggregation of data into triangles derives a model's elevation, slope, aspect, and surface area. The data-generated representation more accurately converts the idiosyncrasies of a geological surface into irregularly distributed nodes and lines of three-dimensional coordinates. Ultimately, this offers a flexible arrangement of non-overlapping triangles, or a triangulated irregular network (TIN). As such, the surface employs faceting triangulation to define a building in BIM at a different scale to both geology and geography.

The (curiously named) *Jackson 5* TIN mappings created by Sandra Lach Arlinghaus, Adjunct Professor of Mathematical Geography and Population–Environment Dynamics at University of Michigan, reveals a noteworthy abstraction of information pertaining to Jackson, Mississippi. Her mapping couples multiple nested surfaces, each with their corresponding triangular facets. Her research correlates surface color and shading to alternative data sets, including the Environmental Protection Agency's online hazardous site locations, Census and United States Geological Surveys, and other boundary-specific information pertaining to animal movement. The map dismisses a conventional architectural interpretation of site and instead provides alternative strategies for interpolation and commentary on where and when (within a chosen Z-value) architectural ideas will occur.

The potential for data interpretation to disrupt the stability of architectural projection constitutes production rooted in deformity itself. Alternative influences of representation, like industrial design cutaway or exploded para-line drawing, can articulate building form and function through dissected "chunks." Analogous to cartographic way-finding, the architect peels away pieces of the building in order to expose critical moments that a project indexes as a whole. This form of visualization accrues detail with a more expansive focus than imagery based on building element isolation. The *Limn Bio-mechanoid Dwellings* project, a drawing study produced by a student team from the Southern California Institute of Architecture (SCI-ARC), uses effects of chiaroscuro, hatching, and projection to create the drawings of a building model with simulated depth and detail. The building, as rendered, deceives with its unbroken hatch pattern that serves as skin articulation. The pattern lines start as a surface texture like corduroy and continue through their geo-massing to become a thinly delineated structure – creating what

Map overlays of Jackson, Mississippi (image courtesy of Arlinghaus)

ON PAGES 132–133
Limn Bio-mechanoid Dwellings (image courtesy of Daniel Karas et al.)

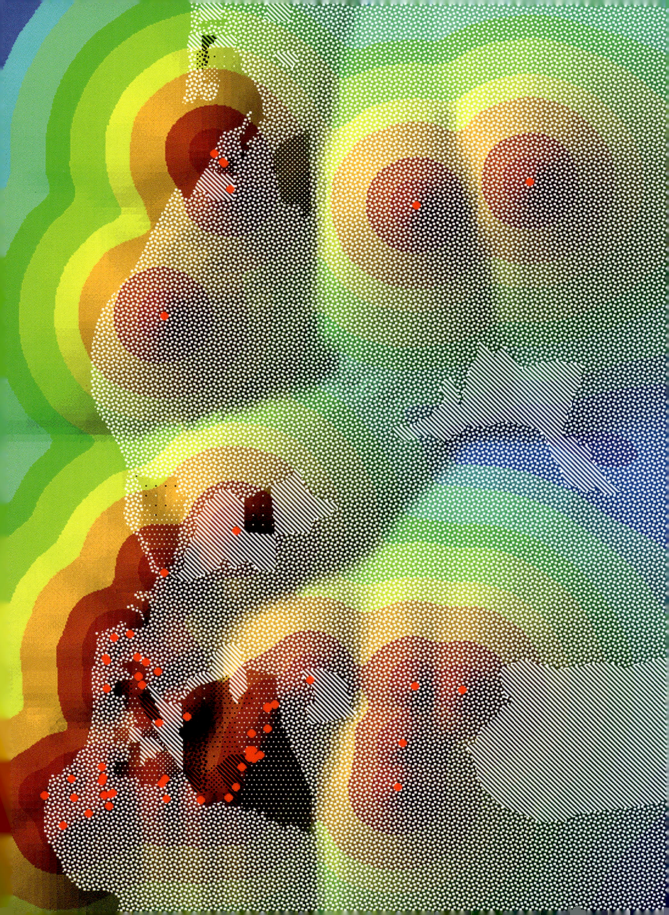

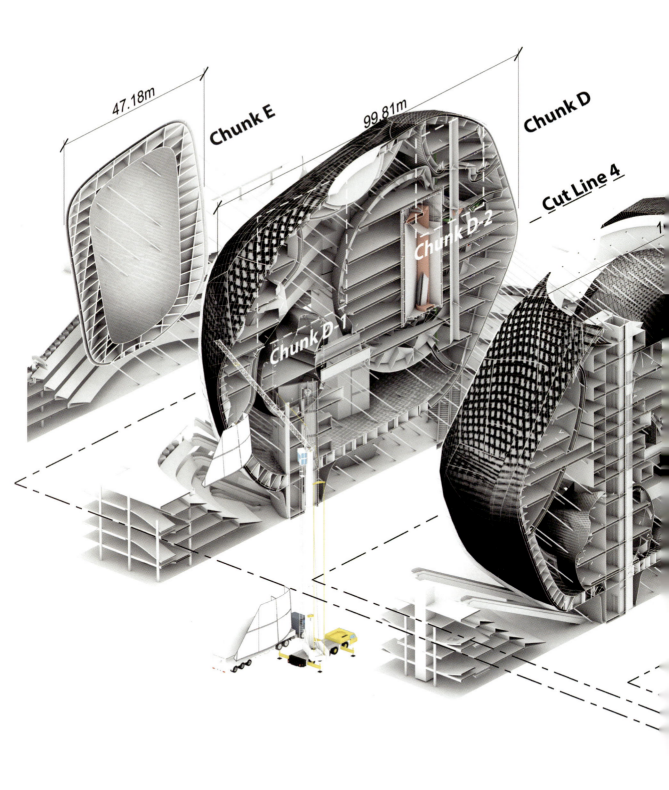

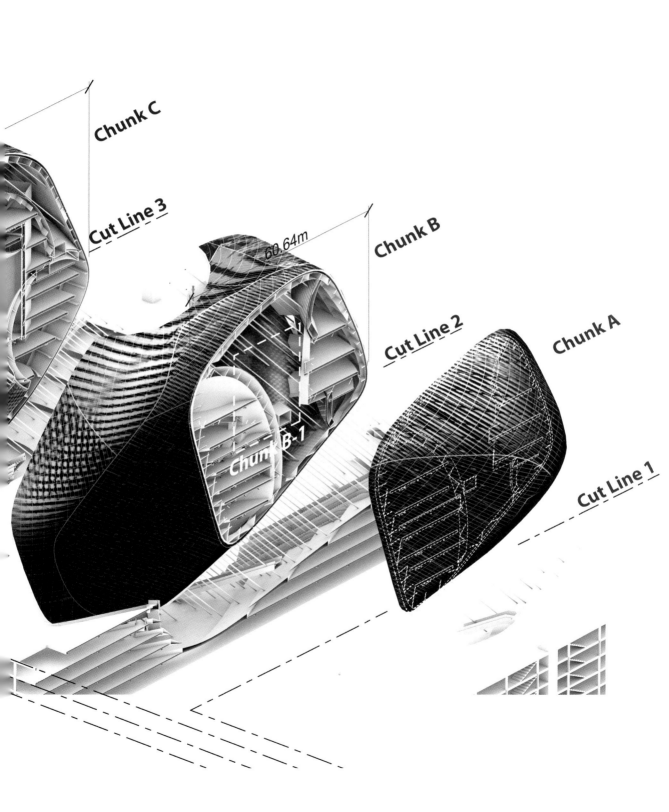

SCI-ARC graduate Danny Karas referred to as a "building as drawing" approach.[6] The chiaroscuro effect accentuates the convex shape and offers up an object with a more or less blank exterior and projected edge to explore its "special cut" sections and chunk-like details. In essence, *Limn* exploits Imhof's visualization strategies along with the idea of a building database, and re-projects itself through multiple geo-conditions.[7] Rather than criticizing BIM's normative "building-ness," the project revels in the very idea of "plausibility." As much as *Limn* appears to adhere to BIM's literal application, its strictures of form and logic truly manifest BIM's as-yet untapped capacity for design innovation.

Oslo Opera House by Snohetta Architects (image courtesy of Iwan Baan)

Surface terrain

In geology, a "suture" is the place where two dissimilar plates join, butting against each other in friction. Typically, a suture results in extraordinary topographic formations that can be miles wide or as small as a step. For architecture, a "suture" interrogates junctions of surface detail, building placement, and the nature of enclosure. This approach usually engenders the less normative details of artificial terrain, such as the roof surface of Snohetta's *Oslo Opera House* in Norway. The sloping surface serves multiple functions: cultural monument, views to the city beyond, and municipal park ground – all of which prompt the building to become an active part of its surroundings. The hand-cut stone cladding is configured into triangular sutures that butt-up and lift ever so slightly to control water drainage. The carefully considered, non-repetitive slab cuts, ledges, and textures, are all based on a pattern generated by local artists and the opinions of more than 70,000 citizens. The landform roof creates the visual impression of an iceberg rising out of the Akerselva River, which flows through and around Oslo as if an addition of new geographical context has arrived.

Snohetta's *Opera House* also engages the suture that occurs where land, sea, and building meet – providing another formal implication from geology that challenges the "ground" upon which architects can reliably build. Such a monumental commitment to geomimetic form requires corresponding effort by its geo-technical engineers. Here, a collaboration with the Norwegian Geotechnical Institute (NGI) offered Snohetta crucial design control in areas of uncertainty. Sitting on 28,000 meters of piles that embed into a thick layer of supportive clay, the 50-meter excavation to bedrock required various domains

of expertise, from the NGI engineers that devised extensive sheet pile cut-off walls and even a ship collision barrier, to the professional divers who performed underwater concrete casting. Kjell Karlsrud, NGI's Expert Adviser on the project, says the precautionary advice against such extreme earthworks for the half-landed disposition was not followed.[8] The boldness of the project's design springs from its actual location and placement on the project ground surface – a factor important enough for the architects to counter the NGI's advice. This decision on the part of Snohetta reinforces the criticality required in situations of collaboration between experts – one that integrated project delivery (IPD), or the process of collaboratively harnessing the talents and insights of all participants to optimize project results – is said to mitigate.[9] In this case, forced design conviction increased value to the owner and maximized the potency of the design, fabrication, and construction rather than the compromises potentially set forth by collaboration.

Within the BIM environment, one method for blanketing a new surface would be to incorporate contextual information. Using proximate geological features from the existing terrain, a speculative design project at the University of Auckland derived data from Ferdinand von Hochstetter's 1864 map of the Auckland volcanic field. First published in the *Geological and Topographical Atlas of New Zealand*, Hochstetter's map reveals a wide array of geographic and geological features – perhaps most interestingly the 53 extinct volcanoes that define domains or neighborhoods in the Auckland metropolitan region. Questions of how the city's urbanites navigate these features prompted a proposal for a series of artificial and active terrains. The geographic features themselves suggest and inspire the particularities of the new terrain design choices in a general mimetic way. By that, the artificial terrain is always a reflection of and response to the actual.

As a gesture toward urban improvement, such a network aspires to link volcano districts through paths of activity and nodes of rest. This design approach to a grounded surface condition often relies on the enigmatic flexibility of its components, particularly with regard to any assertions afforded by the parametric definition. A parameter in this scenario defines the relevant data set coming from the physical terrain, such as the height of the component edge to the actual surface it rests on. The system identifies the range of values that the geometry can act in response to and reference.

GIS/BIM component relative to geological volcano context of New Zealand (image courtesy of Herman Haringa, School of Architecture and Planning, the University of Auckland, Master of Architecture (Professional) Advanced Design 2 Studio, Visiting Professor Danelle Briscoe)

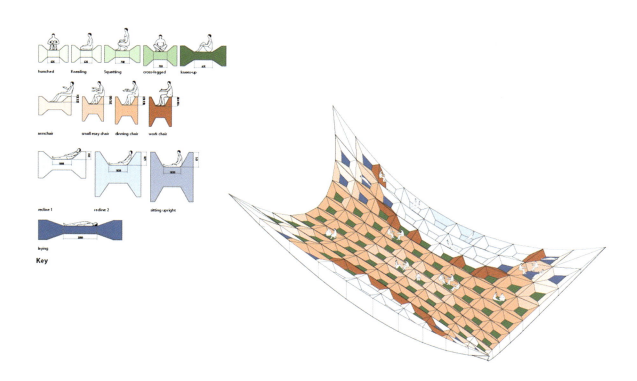

Key

hunched | Kneeling | Squatting | cross-legged | knees-up
armchair | small easy chair | dinning chair | work chair
recline 1 | recline 2 | sitting upright
laying

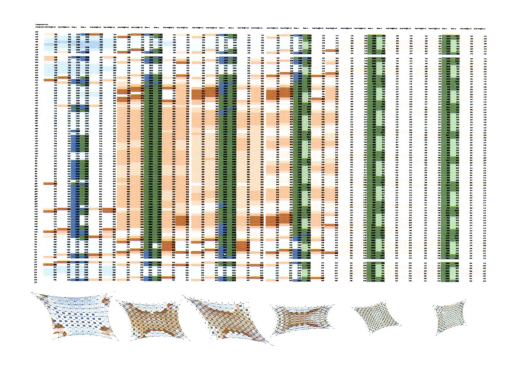

The spacing and quantity of the "beds" promote walkability of urban space between the points by connecting ten-minute increments from one geo-condition to the next. These nodes vary in size and shape as they adapt to the conditions between volcanoes. Subsequently, the ergonomic programs intended for the individual (sitting, chatting, lounging, etc), in combination with essential inner-city landscape surfaces (benches, phone chargers, and water fountains), propose a creative solution to the provisional services necessary for a city's walkability factor. By connecting "best fit" BIM components, a smooth function is constructed that approximates the exact data from millions of comma separated value (CSV) location points. Establishing architectural constraints for placement, geography, and geological proximities, this geometry articulates adaption itself. These multiple – and sometimes conflicting – design conditions can be drawn together spatially, and quantified for design purposes.

Deep structure

John McPhee claims in his non-fiction book, *Assembling California*, "one must develop a talent for 'seeing through the topography' and into the rock on which the topography was carved."[10] The same can be said for the architect trying to suture a building surface to its surrounding topography. In order to combine complexities of site with building surface, a designer must construct a 3D mental map of existing terrain alongside an escalation of structural involvedness – a visualization and tectonic agenda that BIM readily supports.

The *Harbin Cultural Island*, by MAD Architects, conforms to the rolling shoreline of the Songhua River in northern China. The surrounding wetland habitat extends for miles and fuels the project's disposition to blend disparate land features into a cohesive whole. An expansive landscape, the entire project covers an area of 1,800,000 square meters, with a construction area of 79,000 square meters. As a park, the surface offers visitors a panoramic view of the surrounding Songhua River wetland as they walk along the building's highest point. The building's surfaces – custom pure-white aluminum cladding with white stone and concrete pathways – mix and mingle to visually correspond to the site conditions of ice and snow, enabling design control to figuratively traverse the natural topography. The sinuous movement of the building's form strategically reduces its visual impact and directs the flow of people

The *Harbin Cultural Island* rendering (image courtesy of MAD)

ON PAGES 140–141
The *Harbin Cultural Island* under construction (image courtesy of MAD)

from multiple directions to the entrances of its primary programs: the theater and recreation center.

For MAD Architects, BIM enhances their control of construction quality for complex forms, particularly when managing structural technique. Ma Yansong, one of three MAD Principals, firmly believes in generating design from a concept. "Rather than focusing on the technology that enables it, or any parameter theory that drives it," Yansong states, "MAD remains true to design intuition and believes a unique design concept leads to unique design form."[11] Data and information modeling techniques, however, are the primary tools that helped the designers realize their concept. Yansong admits "A data set, unique to each project's internal factors, makes possible the infinite and specific customization based on myriad factors that were never possible to manage prior to BIM." For instance, the *Cultural Island* structure has over 19,000 unique panels, 17,800 of which are curved. This type of conditional and contextual design is the product (in part) of BIM capabilities whereby the project panels and their characteristics are consequential to the organization afforded by material take-off scheduling. In this sense, the BIM process of logistics for structural management heightens design geometry as it inspires confidence in its realization.

In this process of high articulation, the architect specializes rather than generalizes. The virtual modeled environment renders a single vision to direct and constrain building components. These building components are charged with various properties, rather than restricted to purely the geometry of its form. The sentiment that BIM holds with the promise that "one model can do it all!" is not always the case. 3XN, an award-winning Danish architectural practice headquartered in Copenhagen, manipulates a building's form to shape user behavior, and has done so in crafting a single, continuous metal surface for the *Blue Planet Aquarium*. The building carves into the terrain, following the shape of the land, and its faceted form gestures visitors inside. In the end, a considerable catalog of informational data has the potential to shape the building form.

Formally, the project's client wanted a building that could adapt over time to host the evolving world-class aquarium's features and attractions – a process in constant flux since its successful inauguration in 2013. In this way, the building can expand when necessary, adding square meters out into the site and yet remain consistent with the logic

The Blue Planet Aquarium entry view (image courtesy of 3XN/Adam Moerk)

ON PAGES 144–145
The Blue Planet Aquarium under construction (image courtesy of 3XN/Adam Moerk)

and language of its natural context and design concept. Hosting many complex programs with technological requirements for managing water of various temperatures and salinities, the form spirals to a central reference foyer that allows visitors to always end up in the same place, no matter which direction they set off to experience the aquarium.

Because of a client mandate, the *Blue Planet* project was entirely carried out using BIM. In hindsight, Ulrich Pohl, Design Architect for 3XN and the *Blue Planet*, claims the firm learned a great deal about sharing and organizing BIM files from this highly complex project. On one hand, BIM facilitated flexible collaboration with various fields of engineering and their individual data requirements, such as fluid dynamics analysis requiring a precise "waterproof" model divided into 330 segments to achieve wind load calculations on each individual face. On the other hand, when charged with the optimization and construction of the outer shell, Pohl claims BIM allowed mass customization for various unique structural elements, but also meant using various types of software platforms to gain its tangible potential. Rapid design and production of secondary elements, like stair variations, façade patterns, and door selections, also meant an awareness that the coordinated models were always up to date. Like geologic rocks, BIM elements retain individual histories: date of solidification, environment, disposition, metamorphic character. This has huge potential for maintaining quality control, managing interference and, in later phases of the project, calculating costs.

Conclusion

Architecture, through BIM, can borrow techniques and practices from the geological and geographical sciences to facilitate a new understanding of geomimicry.

By using the likenesses and applicable data sets or data derivation from such alternative sources, architecture is more likely to expand how it resolves issues. In particular, BIM demonstrates the capacity to enhance the technically constructed project, whereby highly complex structures – methodically numbered and assembled – create faceted or curved form indicative of the earth's features. Many assurances are formed with the allowance to technically construct the exact placement and detail in BIM, as it represents to a certain extent what can be expected out in the field. The benefits of these formal strategies place high demands on all stakeholders involved, and with BIM they are ideally engaged from the onset of design. Information can therefore lead to an unconventional approach of spatial analysis that suggests new morphologies for buildings, roads, squares, etc. and representational tools now have a direct influence on the conceptual development of a project and the generation of its form in and of site.

Notes
1. Bernard Cache, *Earth Moves: The Furnishings of Territories* (Cambridge, MA: MIT Press, 1995).
2. David Gissen held this position almost a decade ago ["Architecture's Geographic Turns," *LOG* 12 (2008): 59–67].
3. http://archurbanist.blogspot.com/2008/09/geo-mimicry.html (retrieved July 14, 2014).
4. Buckminster Fuller, *Ideas and Integrities: A Spontaneous Autobiographical Disclosure* (New York, NY: Collier, 1969), p. 139.
5. www.bfi.org/about-fuller/big-ideas/dymaxion-world/dymaxion-map (retrieved October 14, 2014).
6. Danny Karas, email to the author, September 16, 2014.
7. These data are derived through IBL shapes in 3D software. The IBL is a moveable point of illumination on a spherically mapped image.
8. Kjell Karlsrud, email to the author, August 25, 2014. As most of the design work took place in 2003–2004, BIM in its current iteration was not used during the design process for the Opera House.
9. The American Institute of Architects (AIA) and AIA California Council, *Integrated Project Delivery: A Guide*. Version 1, 2007 (www.aia.org/ipdg).
10. John McPhee, *Assembling California* (New York, NY: Farrar, Straus & Giroux, 1993), p. 27.
11. Yansong Ma, email to the author, June 19, 2014.

Bibliography
Allen, Stan. "From the Biological to the Geological." In *LandForm Building*, ed. Stan Allan and Marc McQuade. Princeton, NJ and Zurich: Princeton University School of Architecture and Lars Muller, 2011.
Arlinghaus, S. "A Map of Jackson, Mississippi." *Solstice: An Electronic Journal of Geography and Mathematics* X, No. 2.
Guallart, Vicente. *Geologics: Geography Information Architecture*. Barcelona: Actar, 2008.
Harvey, David. "Geographical Reason." In *Cosmopolitanism and the Geographies of Freedom*. New York, NY: Columbia University Press, 2009.

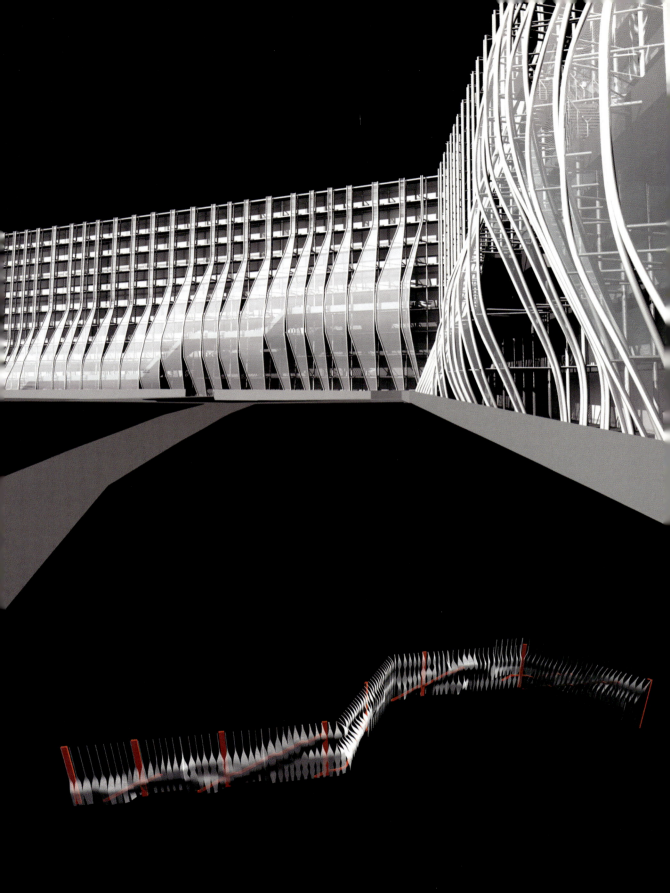

[INTERVIEW]

Greg Lynn
GREG LYNN FORM

BIM techniques have gained the reputation of being a directive toward more normative conditions of form creation, and to some extent provoking a more restrained approach to architectural design. Has BIM (or data-driven process in general) enabled or inhibited your design process?

I think in my experience, which is not necessarily the norm, BIM was initially implemented on formally exotic construction problems to rationalize difficult cases. Because it made difficult things possible and buildable, BIM gained traction on the things that would have been difficult, or even impossible, to do otherwise. Once everyone, from the architects, to the engineers, to the fabricators, to the builders, observed projects that would have been unbuildable being realized with reasonable budgets and time frames, they realized how profitable BIM could be to "business as usual" projects. I think it just says more about the field than it does about BIM. I do not think the field has ever been as risk averse as it is presently and the margins are smaller and smaller for trying to do something new. So because people are not taking risks, there is not a whole lot of profit in any of it. I think we are seeing most innovation today being applied to trying to squeeze a little bit out of a thing which is not so ambitious or innovative.

Can you speak to a project where you might have used BIM in the initial design phase?

The *Kleiburg Housing Block* project was an interesting time because we started off using Maya and the Expression Editor in order to write short MEL scripts for modeling. We were looking at different configurations of neighborhoods in a 500-unit housing block based on stair, escalator, and elevator cores. As we were constantly moving vertical circulation elements around, we realized it was going to be a lot quicker to build a tool rather than remodeling them over

Transformation of *Kleiburg Housing Block* (image courtesy of Greg Lynn)

and over. So we built an Expression Editor that would let us move landing points for all these cores. It would then model a series of architectural elements from landings and corridors to a new truss structure tied to the existing building. It was a BIM approach but we were using Maya. Robert Aish, who was then head of development at Bentley, would come to the office every 3–4 months, and look at what we were doing. I showed him what I was using Maya for and he said he was creating some similar procedural modeling tools for Foster's office. So three months goes by and he comes back with a custom BIM tool for the *Kleiburg* project. Along with some of Foster's *Gherkin* custom tools, this became the start of Smart Geometry suite for Bentley. For me, it was starting with a design concept and then creating a tool to solve it. It started with all the typical details that we were discussing with engineers for construction. That's still probably the one and only time that from a very initial design phase we were using a BIM approach.

Sociopolis Housing Block color study (image courtesy of Greg Lynn)

You are noted to have coined the term "blob architecture" in 1995 with the use of animation software. Having close to two decades of buildings that articulate new formalisms, what geometry does BIM afford?

I've spent a lot of time with Patrick Schumacher and Zaha and the idea of parametricism is very interesting and powerful today; it comes out of an approach to form and detail that I find very Modern and Germanic. BIM has always been about promoting a high degree of articulation. What's funny about "blob" architecture is that I've never regretted using a word as much as that word. I remember the late Ernest Pascucci, then the editor of *Any* magazine, was pushing me to use the term very explicitly. I kept responding: "it's just the name of a software technique, blob modeler." It allowed me to take discrete spheres and merge them into clay-like volumes. I could add detail by simply adding more of these spheres. It was unlike a spline model where every time I wanted to add a feature, I had to re-loft the entire surface. It was procedural in a new way. What was a surprise to me was that journalists really picked up on the term and it got to be associated with very primitive computer renderings where detail was absent and surfaces appeared somewhat slick, shiny and featureless. It had more to do with the fact that we were amateur renderers and didn't know how to put a lot of information in a

rendering. Everything BIM is the reverse. Two decades later, what you see is a celebration of articulation on very similar geometries to the blob. There is not anything implicit about it. I think Patrick's argument about parametricism is highly theorized, but the focus on architecture being an assembly of components and celebrating each one of those component connections, I find to be a very old idea.

Along that line, there is a current trend of buildings to rest staunchly on, in, or like the ground or landforms they mimic (spelled out by Allen & McQuade's *Landform Building*). Does this formalism suggest a new position from the assurances of BIM based on a reciprocity between building elements and form?

I think you could put in a category of new difficult problems getting solved by an approach to construction by the architect. With all the geometric sophistication and research, when the geometry becomes tectonic, it falls into the clear tectonic categories that BIM modelers and managers promote. That's the one argument I have with Patrick [Schumacher]. That tectonic legacy of primary structure, secondary structure, skin, and shading really gets reinforced and curiously it creates a lot of redundancies. It is taking architecture wildly out of step with other design fields where you see a reduction of components and elements doing more than one function. Composites, gluing, and other trends of assembly have nothing to do with maximizing components or their mechanical connections. It might still be more efficient to have all those redundancies in the field of architecture that is out of step with other construction fields because of tolerances and methods of assembly acceptable in a building.

Can you comment on the formalism of the façade design for the *Sociopolis Housing Block* project? What is the building information that the facets and color coding address?

I've always tended toward facets, like with the *Korean Presbyterian Church* of New York, more so than with continuous curved surfaces. With that language and the metal building skin of the *Sociopolis*, every tenth panel is a window. When we built the first physical model, the punched openings were very Flintstone looking. The plan was to take the aluminum panels and anodize them in one of six colors. It was based on something Peter Eisenmann did when I worked for him in the 1980s, where he wanted a model to be painted to look like a *Tron* rendering. We painted each face of the model in a slightly different shade of the same color, and it looked like it was digitally shaded. In the *Sociopolis* façade this was done by digital means; all the panels in shadow are dark black anodized; those in shade are gold or bronze; those in sun are polished silver or white. We did a crude shading pass and then assigned one of these six colors to the surfaces to take the whammy off the window panels.

For your SUPRASTUDIO taught at UCLA, you note CNC elements described through BIM as being an "industry standard." If we can assume that academy leads industry and not the other way around, how should academia push new relationships of CNC, BIM, or the relationship between the two?

It is interesting that BIM is the one place where the academy has not led the field. It is anathema to students and faculty to use it. I have heard academics and practitioners be very derogatory about schools that teach it within the curriculum. When people go into offices, the same way they used to say "I don't want to be the one drafting bathroom details and wall sections," now they are saying "I don't want to work at that place because I'll just be stuck on *Revit*™." It has yet to be exploited and experimented with in the academy in the way it probably could or should and I don't necessarily know why that is. It entered into things to expedite repetitive drafting tasks, but it does a lot more than that and I think anybody invested in how something is going to get made, assembled, and transported gets into BIM questions quickly.

I had the pleasure of hearing you and Bill Kreysler speak at ACADIA 2012 in San Francisco. I believe you collaborated on the *Bloom House* in 2010, a time when BIM had gathered a bit of maturity and momentum. How did BIM play into this project or consultant collaborations (if at all)?

With Bill especially, we will prototype at full or quarter scale to understand how something is going to be made and to convince a contractor. I tend to do that physically and then reverse engineer

Sociopolis Housing Block reflective study (image courtesy of Greg Lynn)

a BIM approach from a physical assembly study. With the Bloom House there were three construction methods that we invented (invention may be too strong a term, but at least we were ignorant of alternatives). One was the curved walls which were all framed with diagonally interlocking laser-cut plywood framing. We did a one-third scale test and built a big chunk of it. We saved quite a bit of cost over balloon framing. We were building the physical mockup and then building the software afterward to expedite the labor for documentation to make the walls. We had the shapes in plan and a couple of details explaining how to assemble them, mostly so we could number everything. But in terms of shop drawings and fabrication, we completely cut the contractor out. We even found the company that did all the laser-cutting, so the contractor was just a pass-through for accounting. The other thing was all the Corian wet surfaces in the kitchen and bathrooms were custom developed with Dupont. We were producing all fabrication information and some of the mold-making samples ourselves, and if not we were sending the geometry directly to Dupont's fabrication shop in Buffalo. There was very little drawn and just bubbled notes around these elements with a note that said "Not in contractor's scope."

What are your thoughts on the afterlife (or life-cycle) of a BIM model? Do you imagine (or are you currently) incorporating BIM facilities maintenance on any projects through post-occupancy?

So far I have never had a client ask for all those services, but it has been discussed. What is more relevant with our work is mobile furniture and building robotics into spaces. The real challenge there is how we document a space that will contain a moving thing. The new Google phone is one approach that could be used to build a fairly quick 3D file of this space. Every time you add something, or the robot moves, it updates itself, like a self-driving car. But those data don't have any other information attached to them, whereas a BIM model not only has material, it has dates, ownership, etc., and is a much more robust approach. I think if architects were more entrepreneurial and seeing that we have a way to deliver a data management service or 3D database approach to retailers or stadiums, there would be a huge appetite for it. Instead, it is more about people's anxiety about exposure or 3D file sharing due to liability. I think this could have a significant impact on architects and their geometry.

Jim Denevan drawing, *Lake Biakal*, Siberia (image courtesy of Peter Hinson, 2010)

7

BIM landscape

There are many notable instances in which architects and landscape architects have collaborated efficiently throughout the design process. Nonetheless, BIM offers a pivotal environment that can further these collaborations through greater ease and effectiveness: easier in that a unified model provides a cohesive and concurrent representation of the design and associated meta-data; and more effective in that a shared model enables the performance of landscape and building to be analyzed as a complete system. The use of alternative information types coming from the reciprocating disciplines of architecture and landscape architecture broaden the range and domain of the information model and its application, consequently resulting in new forms of design representation and outcome. In return, this alternative thinking suggests new ways to model, inform, and construct landscape – a relationship made possible through the scale and scope of ideas grounded in the objective facts of an information model.

The use of BIM particular to the design of landscape brings together "land" which exists as a quantifiable entity to what can inform the "scape" in which site and data converge. The land and the built environment coexist through pattern application or from natural systems and the varying surfaces that now befit a canvas for data translation into physical output. As extreme as the dry lakes of Lake Biakal, Siberia, pattern overlaid with the aid of a Global Position System (GPS) offers Jim Denevan, the artist responsible for scribing the snow and sand in the *Lake Biakal* project, the boundary conditions to implement design onto (what he calls) "drawable space."[1] For Denevan, different boundaries suggest different visual solutions and, in the case of *Lake Biakal*, data constraint manifests in the form of natural occurrence, such as extremely low snowfall (i.e., about two or two inches for an entire winter). What was anticipated to be a relatively stable drawing context became a condition of forced excavation due to unusually high snowfall that season. The resultant pattern points to the condition of data accuracy overlaid with a lack of assuredness of natural systems that landscape architecture must constantly contend with and attempt to quantify.

GIS to BIM

Landscape architects typically harvest data from geographic information systems (GIS). Having its introduction in the early 1960s by renowned landscape architect and academic Ian McHarg, the development of a parallel track between GIS and landscape design was not reliant on technology. McHarg's use of graphic matrices categorized numbers, quantities, facts, and pure data for the purpose of rapid intercompatibility of land uses alongside determinant and consequential design agendas.[2] His research established the use of tabular information, such as a colorful graph form as representation for the design of the built environment. As an information type, GIS now offers a noteworthy file translation to BIM that identifies and extracts spatial factors, ranging from demographics to environmental analysis depending on the scope of a project.[3]

In part, the current incorporation and increased use of GIS to BIM is a result of the availability of geospatial data itself. The release of Google Earth in 2005 transformed the ease with which one can access GIS data through synchronized Google data, making it ubiquitous to the point where users typically are unaware they are even accessing it.[4] The scale of information from GIS and BIM greatly differs, as each foci originates at opposite ends of the spectrum, from the global view of Earth to the hyper-local conditions of a building element, respectively. The constant conflation of global to local space, however, causes an intermingling of scales that creates a new design perspective from which architects see the world. It has precipitated a fundamental change in the notions of context and proximity.

Using space-based satellite navigation, such as GPS, BIM provides an added spatial dimension and exactitude to the design analysis process and extends further downstream to building management. GIS stores and manipulates the data that GPS accumulates, thus extending the building model to the specifics of its site and allowing the design process to more precisely address landscape, or architecture, or both simultaneously. The ability to query the location of cultural and economic assets and to ascertain how these assets might be efficiently sited, distributed, or maintained becomes an exciting basis for form generation.

Design matrix from *Design with Nature,* developed by Ian McHarg for prospective land use and degree of compatibility (image courtesy of Wiley Press)

ON PAGES 160–161
GIS/BIM spatial diagram (image provided by Danelle Briscoe with Zach Walters)

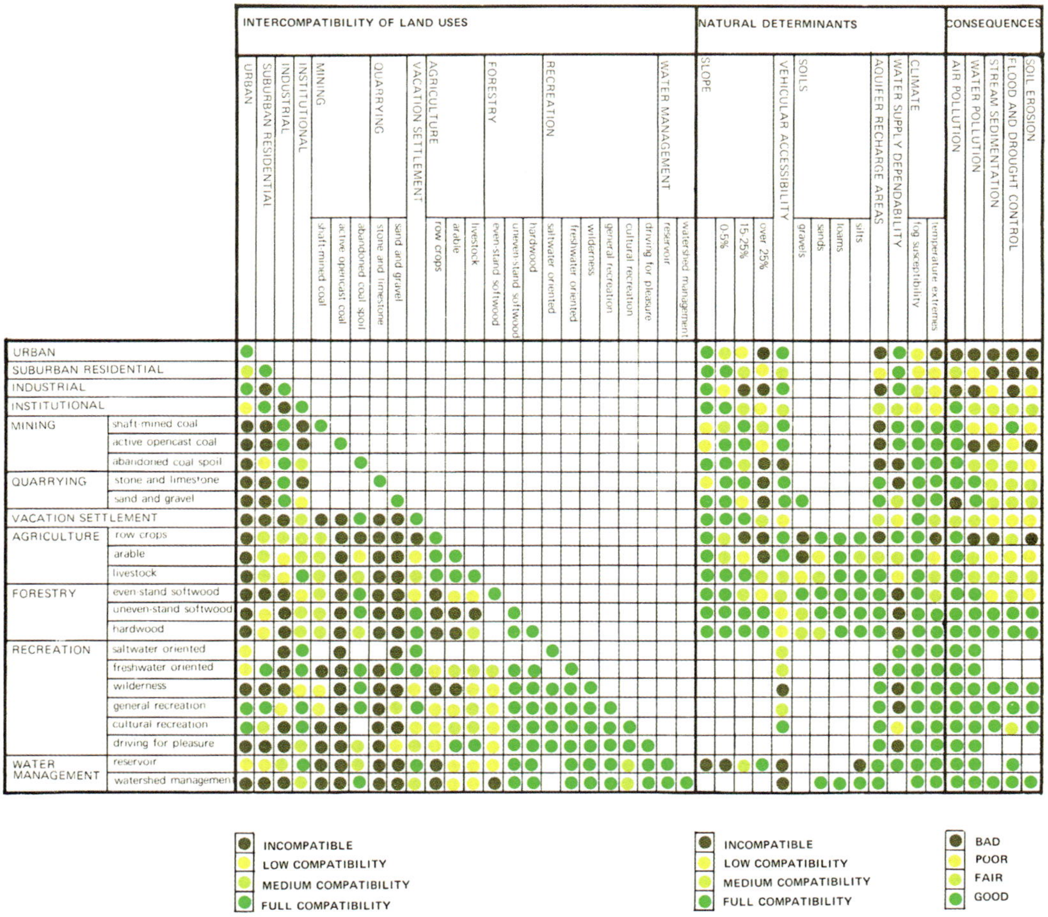

DEGREE OF COMPATIBILITY

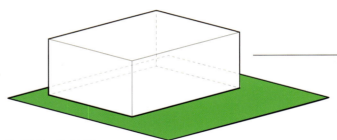
Real Property Asset

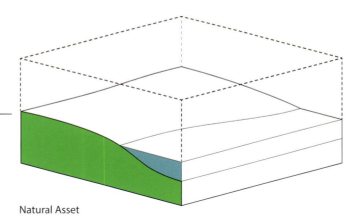
Natural Asset

GIS Space

BIM Space

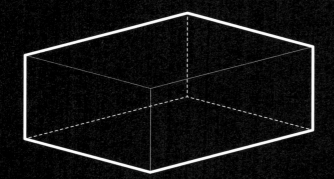

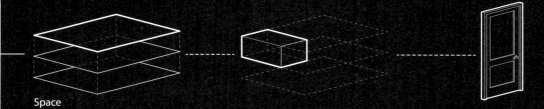
Space

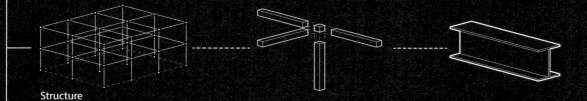
Structure

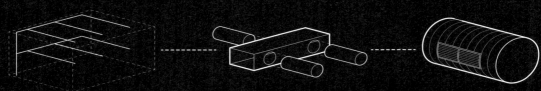
System

Hoosier Energy Headquarters, BIM Planting Plan completed in 2014 (image courtesy of Lauren Schmidt)

BIM to LIM

Although historically landscape architecture has engaged technology, the discipline has currently by and large resisted the leap into BIM. Unlike architecture, landscape surfaces are hardly ever flat and often slope in multiple directions and more often than not, planting regions tend toward organic profiles. Creating sinuous landscape forms or smooth grading can be a challenge given the limitations of the tools and existing component libraries that are reputedly not geared toward landscape interventions nor designed to meet the various conditions of site work. Therefore, much of their work still relies on diagrammatic design strategies to assert the quantitative and qualitative effects of relationships to site.

BIM content nevertheless can be found for nearly every CSI category associated with landscape architecture (masonry, specialties, lighting, exterior improvements, etc.) and many landscape-specific components already exist in all BIM libraries and standards. Plants, bollards, tree grates, or parking spaces can be placed and tallied automatically. In most cases, highly detailed content can be found, but more complex entities, such as the curbs, cuts, and curved walls, are also easily created or acquired. Using the same capabilities within BIM that architects use to design floor systems can be hacked for the build-up layers of roads, rails, or large-scale site modeling. Other (more extensive) content resides in the National BIM Library, such as the *Plug Planted Extensive Green Wildflower Roof System* that models and specifies full packages of plant types and building system composites.[5] The design and layout of these standard landscape features and objects can leverage the database underpinnings to associated specifications, details, manufacturer data, etc. Such elements add to the potentially integrated delivery of simulation, visualization, and analysis of landscape architecture.

In planning for both hard and soft landscape elements, BIM can be used to store data for landscape architects to easily develop and organize ground pattern and arrangement with many details involved. The planting plan for *Hoosier Energy Headquarters* in Bloomington, Indiana demonstrates how a landscape model enables the designer to plan the layout and importantly report the proposal. Landscape soft elements such as different plant types, pot size, and water usage combine information with hard elements such as lighting, surface covering, and walk pathways. Lauren Schmidt, founder and author of *landarchBIM* blog and former Graduate Landscape Architect working on this plan for

Schmidt Associates, sees it as a particularly good example of using BIM in landscape architecture to create custom data sets. She states:

> For budgetary reasons, a majority of the plants had to be split into an alternate bid. By simply adding a parameter to all plants and plant areas, this data was quickly and easily conveyed in both the plant schedules and all plant tags (note the alternate indicator <A> in the tags). In addition, custom formulas allow all areas to automatically calculate the correct plant count based on a specified spacing. Both of these data sets resulted in substantial time savings during the documentation process.[6]

Further activation of this well-developed BIM landscape plan would simply require tagging each allocated plant symbol placed with more data input, such as their specific water needs in order to monitor or record site-wide consumption.[7]

Landscape conditions are often more field than object, and so resist being reduced to the boundary representations used in most modeling environments. For example, the compaction or saturation of soils is a diffuse gradient as compared to a brick that possesses distinct limits and relatively uniform material properties. Moreover, the aesthetics and performance of most landscape systems must be assessed over time and in relation to the other systems with which they interact. In his visualization *Landscape Information Modelling*, Philip Belesky, researcher and designer from the Royal Melbourne Institute of Technology/Spatial Information Architecture Laboratory (SIAL), asserts that this dynamic data diagram can be an effective means of representing site conditions and its cyclical nature, as well as serve as a model for automatically generating the design of detailed planting schemes. The graph represents a computational design process that analyzes the conditions of two plant species within a specific estuarine area. An individual plant can be selected according to the soil type that matches its particular preferences and the active "drawing" then places a series of species together according to their tolerance of water-saturated soils, from high to low tolerances. Belesky cautions that the demonstrated snapshot is merely a visualization of the current state of one aspect of one system at one particular moment in time.

Particularly within a landscape context, it is necessary to understand how a single representational tool gives evidence of the forces of an

Landscape Information Modelling (image provided by Philip Belesky)

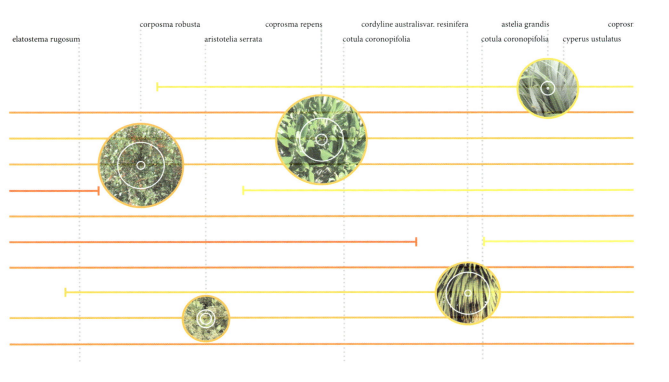
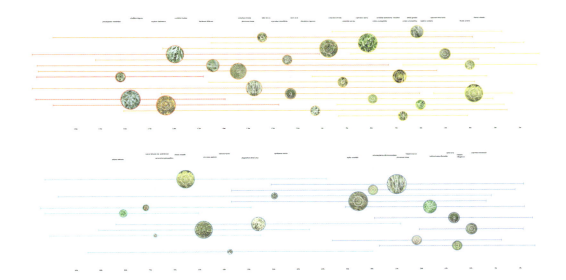

underlying system, how that system interacts with other systems, and how both those forces and interactions will evolve over time. Belesky claims: "The challenges of system interaction need to be met if the performances of landscape are to be analyzed with the same fidelity as buildings."[8] For conceptualization, Belesky has created this custom version of Landscape Information Modeling (or LIM), but he more so values the BIM environment in the later stages of the design process, when more rigorous resolutions of design details are required. This position regarding current BIM will only transform, in his opinion, when BIM offers landscape architects the full range of benefits that are currently available to architects.

A cross-section of *Consular Walk at the Embassy of the United States*, London, extracted from a building information model developed by KieranTimberlake (Architect), OLIN (Landscape Architect), Arup (MEP and Civil Engineer), and Weidlinger Associates (Structural Engineer) (rendering courtesy of KieranTimberlake/Studio AMD)

BIM collaboration

Integrated design between disciplines is another fundamental aspect toward realizing the best possibilities for the building and site program. Laurie Olin is one of the landscape profession's most renowned practitioners and educators. His firm, OLIN, boldly used BIM on a pilot project in 2011 to continue their quest for new ways to design, collaborate, and visualize.

Partner Richard Roark maintains:

> Technologically speaking, BIM has helped aid integrated design but it is limited by what it can reveal. Current platforms are object biased and lend themselves toward fixed structures versus dynamic and fluid materials. As we move forward in the refinement of software for design and engineering we must shift the perspective from the discrete identity of objects to their behavior in environments. Landscape architects are working with dynamic materials and externalities that the building envelope's typical function is to resist. To further the potential of sustainable development we need to develop media platforms that allow us to model and share the information of living systems and their associated affects with the building. The ability to model changes for such factors as hydrologic volumes and rates, wind intensity, heat gain and transpiration of plant materials, solar intensity, and light porosity can only be modeled with extreme computational demand that remains by and large aspirational, yet is essential to practice.[9]

Even though creating each element in the model as a unique instance can be time consuming and laborious during concept and

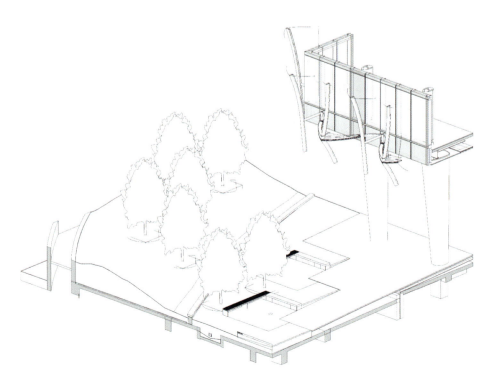

schematic stages, OLIN Project Designer Jessica Henson finds true value in the extraction of information from the BIM model. She claims:

> "Projects with landscapes on top of their structure (i.e. green roof) or projects with complex site/building interactions lend themselves to a BIM workflow – one that OLIN feels helps understand the design intention of each discipline working on a project."[10]

For the *Consular Walk at the Embassy of the United States* in London, the BIM was developed by Architects KieranTimberlake of Philadelphia to integrate the entire scope of design with the geographically distributed engineering and design disciplines: OLIN (Landscape Architect), Arup (MEP and Civil Engineer), and Weidlinger Associates (Structural Engineer). The project is said to have provided a more streamlined coordination process between this multi-disciplinary and multi-office team, but more importantly, it was a pioneer project for landscape architecture, as well as the coordination of architecture and site design using BIM technology. OLIN developed the site topography, pavement, site wall and intensive green roof systems; linking the architectural model to the site elements for a more cohesive, integrated approach to relating building to ground plane. This specifically enabled the OLIN team to incorporate site improvements using the conflict detection analysis prior to construction. It also facilitated the ability to produce accurate, up-to-date design renderings of the project prior to construction.

In general, the BIM interface supports this high degree of collaboration and coordination because it is an intelligent model. It acts as a knowledge repository and proliferator of specialization from each discipline it involves. The strength of the model relies on the diversity and distribution of a project team and they in return rely on it to have access to the most consistent, coordinated, and accurate project information across all stakeholders. The integrated approach allows each team to create, revise, and share project data in the BIM database on a regular basis and, importantly as these models are shared, they are also being systematically managed and protected. When changes are made to files, a complete version history of all changes is maintained and team members who referenced the object are automatically notified of the update and can refresh their copy to see the changes. In this manner, team members can work collaboratively without fear of overwriting one another's data. Moreover, secure information exchange

Habitat Design for Golden-Cheeked Warbler CSV/BIM component (image courtesy of Angela Yoo, School of Architecture and Planning, the University of Auckland, Master of Architecture (Professional) Advanced Design 2 Studio, Visiting Professor Danelle Briscoe)

Adult 10cm | Pine Oak Forest | Insectivorous | Central Americas Flyway Migration route | Stopover Site

Golden-Cheeked Warbler

Migration
1600 km
150-600m altitude

- **Breeding Territory** — Juniper-Oak Forest, Central Texas
- **Migration Route**
- **Important Stopover** — Pine-Oak Forest, Trans-Mexican Volcanic Belt
- **Non-breeding Range** — Pine-Oak Forest, Northern Nicaragua

- **March - July** — Climate
- **Migration Route**
- **Favourable Weather Conditions / Sufficient Food Resources**
- **Wintering Site** — Climate

safe place to lo... shelter

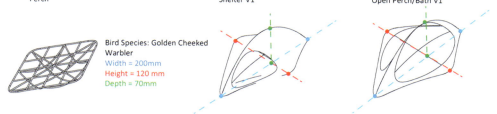

Perch | Shelter V1 | Open Perch/Bath V1

Bird Species: Golden Cheeked Warbler
Width = 200mm
Height = 120 mm
Depth = 70mm

with robust permissions and version control are also becoming more common.[11]

As this collaborative process evolves, so will the increased diversity of information shared, as per Roark's request. The role of living systems, for example the design of a *Habitat for a Golden-Cheeked Warbler*, and their associated effect on the built environment and landscape can conceivably become prioritized in these cooperative scenarios. Detailed CSV data from the Central Flyway Migration destinations integrates building, ecology, and fauna of this particular species and demonstrates engagement with alternative information types, such as GIS and GPS data, as parameters into BIM. In other words, the collaboration could be inclusive of and coordinated to the pressures from flora and fauna.

More recently, value is being added, not only in automating the scheduling of planting plans and collaboration, but also in tracking costs and sourcing landscape materials appropriate to the region. Keyhole Markup Language (KML) file notations can be used to display geographic annotations or visualizations within two-dimensional maps and three-dimensional Google Earth browsers. OLIN has experimented with using associated custom data sets in later phases of the design process such as this function that can geo-locate materials, such as stone from the closest nearby quarries or plants from regional nurseries. This allows a designer to determine whether the desired product is local to the project or more remote. Roark explains, "Our ultimate goal is the development of a reporting system that continuously and fully tracks sustainability and performance metrics as the design is refined." The desire for a user-friendly way to develop materials and landscape libraries with attribute data seems within reach but not quite in hand currently. OLIN is currently using BIM on two new projects in the office and notes an increasing amount of proposals requesting the use of BIM.

Green wall

A green wall, or living wall as it is sometimes called, embodies a vertical building element where architecture and landscape literally merge. This system is architectural in that it delineates building components to hold plant matter and is bounded and supported by architectural form and services. Yet it is also landscape in that the embedded plant growth changes over time and requires an accordance to environmental conditions.[12] The characteristics of an extensive green wall necessitate planning coordination and planting methodologies that challenge the current capabilities of BIM as a design tool.

A database can be manipulated as a design resource to accommodate the appropriate information about plant species for a green wall. In order to generate a plant pattern for the wall, designers create and assign geometry through a BIM component system to contain the plants, as well as shape regions with plant specificity. Every time a model element (i.e., plant type) or its placement is modified, BIM automatically coordinates the change in all views that display that element, but perhaps more importantly the quantification leads to qualification. By scheduling material take-offs of various pattern iterations, information as specific as the planting material's drought tolerance, Lepidoptera linkages or required soil quantities feeds back into the process and flags optimal patterns, potential habitat, or ecological relationships for design team decision-making.[13] To be able to specify, quantify, and then generate a full material takeoff in relation to design means having a live tracking system to validate, or value-engineer, one pattern over the other. Particularly for a vertical wall, this validation shifts the focus of design pattern from primarily one of aesthetics to instead the valued information at hand. Pushing the life cycle of a BIM further, information on a green wall system and plant type can be compelled to generate a post-installation plant maintenance guide from the attributes of the plants within the BIM.

The precision by which BIM can derive data from flora and fauna offers physical building elements (consequential to a modular green wall system) characteristics of site specificity, such as weather data and geography. For the *Caixa Museum* in the temperate climate of Madrid, Spain, Herzog + de Meuron converted a former power station into a visual confrontation between two facing façades. One of these is covered by green plants, creating a vertical garden by Patrick Le Blanc, while the other consists of a Cor-ten steel addition, built on top of the existing brick complex. The perspectival contrast of these planes holds the green wall as a decisive objectile, rather than experiential, element. This position confounds landscape architect and theoretician Diana Balmori's claim that "change in the relationship between architecture and landscape has a lot to do with the fact that space has become more important than the object."[14] In part, the building breaks down boundaries that inherently question whether it is architecture or landscape and how in the end it is a by-product of BIM.

ON PAGES 172–173
Caixa Museum perspective
(image provided by Iwan Baan)

Conclusion

In the field of landscape architecture there is a substantial lack of understanding regarding BIM, be it content, collaboration, or as systems that interact with other systems. Based on open standards and workflows, BIM has provided a universal approach to the collaborative design, realization, and operation of buildings which is increasingly transitioning into a provision for landscape architecture as well. With exemplar projects such as the *Consular Walk*, landscape architecture is considered a key part of this collaborative knowledge base and, as such, must engage the future of BIM.

Data generated from the idiosyncrasies of the "scape" challenge representation and thus generation of site. The pattern coordination relies on controlled scheduling of these conditions, while remaining open to its volatile nature or occurrence over time. The associations between the macro and the micro, from global input views of Earth to the hyper-local conditions of a building element, demonstrate benefits of being inclusive of both. Standard data-gathering tools, such as a GPS tracking system, can be linked to BIM to reconsider the canvas and content known as the landscape. More specifically, the association of plant species to a structural system and materiality can define and support optimal growth performance and functionality – even if it is that of human artifice.

Whether it is BIM or LIM, the landscape discipline is poised for greater application in exploring the unconventional proliferation of information coming from the physical world. The degree to which a database can offer new insight into scalability of "drawable space" lends itself to an even greater design interchange between a building, its site, and the disciplines that control the two.

Notes

1. Jim Denevan, email to the author, May 12, 2014.
2. Ian McHarg, *Design with Nature* (New York, NY: Natural History Press, 1969), pp. 137–152.
3. Jason Sowell, email to the author, April 27, 2014.
4. John Przybyla, "The Next Frontier for BIM: Interoperability with GIS," *Journal of Building Information Modelling* (Fall 2010): 14–18.
5. Extensive green roof systems are composed of grasses and herbaceous perennials with hardy succulents and annuals included to suit individual projects requirements. www.nationalbimlibrary.com/sig-design-and-technology/plug-planted-extensive-green-roof-system-wildflower (retrieved November 28, 2014).
6. Lauren Schmidt, email to the author, December 31, 2014.
7. "Recording Water Consumption of a Planting Plan via Revit," Penn State University Wiki Page, http://bim.wikispaces.com/Recording+Water+Consumption+of+a+Planting+Plan+via+Revit (retrieved December 28, 2014).

8   Philip Belesky, email to the author, July 7, 2014.
9   Richard Roark, interview with the author, July 14, 2014.
10 Jessica Henson, interview with the author, July 27, 2014. Henson notes the frequent use of Civil3D to create TIN surfaces to study topography, slopes, drainage, and slope aspect. This is frequently coordinated with GIS and occasionally GPS data for site analysis. On projects with complex grading, they export TIN files from Civil3D as XML and import them into BIM software. This allows OLIN to be more precise with topography and to easily revise grading using Civil3D.
11 www.synergis.com/uploads/resources/BIMDataManagementandCollaboration.pdf (retrieved December 28, 2014).
12 Philip Belesky, email to the author, July 7, 2014. Belesky commented on green walls and the two disciplines.
13 Danelle Briscoe, "Parametric Planting: Green Wall System Research + Design using. BIM," *Design Agency: Proceedings of the 34th Annual Conference of the Association for Computer Aided Design in Architecture (ACADIA)*, ed. David Gerber, Alvin Huang, and Jose Sanchez (1st edition, Cambridge, Ontario: Riverside Architectural Press, 2015), pp. 333–338.
14 Jared Green, "Interview with Diana Balmori," *The Dirt: Uniting the Built & Natural Environments*, April 11, 2012 http://dirt.asla.org/2012/04/11/interview-with-diana-balmori (retrieved July 28, 2014).

Bibliography

Ahmad, Mohammad and Abdullahi Adamu. "The Need for Landscape Information Modelling (LIM) in Landscape Architecture." 13th Digital Landscape Architecture Conference Proceedings, Bernburg, Germany, June 8, 2013, pp. 531–540.

Allen, Stan. *Landform Building*. Baden: Lars Mueller Publishers, 2011.

Goldman, M. (2011). "Landscape Information Modeling." www.di.net/articles/landscape_information_modeling (retrieved December 28, 2014).

Landscape Institute (2014). "BIM Open Project." www.landscapeinstitute.org/knowledge/BIMOpenProject.php (retrieved March 31, 2014).

Landscape Institute (2014). "What is BIM?" www.landscapeinstitute.org/knowledge/WhatisBIM.php (retrieved March 31, 2014).

Maas, Winy. *Metacity Datatown*. Rotterdam: MVRDV/010, 1999.

McHarg, Ian. *Design with Nature*. New York, NY: Natural History Press, 1969.

Reiser, Jessie, "The Abuse of Data: Map/Territory Confusion," *Atlas of Novel Tectonics*. New York, NY: Princeton Architectural Press, 2006.

[INTERVIEW]

Diana Balmori
BALMORI ASSOCIATES, INC. LANDSCAPE AND URBAN DESIGN

In your book *Landscape Manifesto*, you argue that if architects and landscape architects were on the same page, buildings and landscapes could perform as "linked, interactive systems that heal the environment." Does the information model have the potential to serve as that page? Could a data-driven context unite the two disciplines in the way you imagine?

Yes, a data-driven system could potentially put these disciplines on the same page. But having landscape architects and architects start their work at the same time could achieve this too. The best design process directs ideas from one discipline to the other mainly through discussion at the very start of the project. A project in New York, the *240 Central Park South*, was in my mind a missed opportunity because it was a superficial treatment of a handsome Art Deco building with landmark status. It had already been completely renovated by the time we were called in, there was no chance of intervening in anything that was not the traditional division between architecture and landscape. On the technology side, there are still gaps in how the two disciplines work with data. The architects are not working with GIS, and the landscape architects are working with fewer of the three-dimensional programs.

What does the future hold for practice in terms of technology or data-harvesting?

Data harvesting is all-important: it is the base from which to start. This means that a data-harvesting period needs to take place before design begins and be included in the project fee. This is a struggle, at times.

240 Central Park South landmark building renovation with landscape design by Balmori Associates (image courtesy of Balmori Associates, Inc., photo credit Mark Dye)

Sound Waves diagramming (image courtesy of Balmori Associates, Inc.)

ON PAGES 180–181
New City in Sejong, Korea, to be completed in 2015 (image courtesy of Balmori Associates, Inc., photo credit Efrain Mendez at archframe.net)

During the last 20 years, James Corner and others have developed the concept of data_scape as "constructive and suggestive of new spatial formations . . . objectively constituted (from numbers, quantities, facts, and pure data) to have great persuasive force in the bureaucratic and management maps of conventional planning." This definition begins to give understanding to the creation of a scape — or topography — by means of manipulating data. Do you consider any of your projects to be a data_scape? Or have you developed your own definition?

We designed a temporary garden we call *Sound Waves* in Beijing for the 2012 China International Garden Expo that was all data_scape. The goal was to embody the feelings triggered by viewing nature as depicted in Chinese landscape painting. In our garden design, we reproduced the appearance of the magical Guilin Mountains, located along the Li River. We used bands of planting like three-dimensional brushstrokes to play on the convention of reading topographic contours. Instead of connecting points of equal elevation, the contour lines mapped areas of similar condition.

We constructed a parametric computational model of the garden that performed by subdividing the site into a grid of points, which were then analyzed individually. We analyzed more than 140 points, looking at year-round natural conditions including sun hours per day, slope, altitude, and wind exposure. Plants were selected based on seasonal colors, textures, smells, and their capacity to clean the city's polluted air, and a "standard" index growth pattern for each species was identified, situated, and "scaled" by the computational model to reflect the effect of the various local conditions on the garden's growth. The model thus adapted to the information flow.

Another example is Sejong, the administrative city in Korea, a project won in an international competition. Here we generated all forms through a parametric based on the site's topography. A continuous tangential line (CTL) is a formal principle for generating regulating lines inside the city. Originating in the existing topography, it is intended to provide an endless, three-dimensional seam that acts as a thickened surface between architecture and landscape.

Sejong is an example that demonstrates that by working in conjunction with Haean's A&E subsidiary in New York City from

the start, we were able to completely transform the idea of a green roof. A false terminology in any case, as an idea it can transform the building itself. *Sejong* houses all government buildings (i.e., 21 ministries in 13 buildings) under one superstructure – one that provides a 4k long park for all government staff in their own place of work. The idea that this is an applied green roof is ludicrous; instead it has completely shaped the architecture.

Do you feel that collaborating with others is necessary to produce better healing environments or more holistic projects?

Whether we like it or not, collaboration is the only way to go. We need specialized knowledge from many fields.

What is your means of collaboration, and how has it benefited your projects?

Collaboration means working on a design jointly and within the same time period. If I stress time it is because traditionally landscape architects have been brought in when things such as siting, access roads, and building design have already been decided. By coming into the process late, there is no chance of moving beyond the traditional division between architecture and landscape. This is, I think, an obsolete way of working that produces poor results.

We had a particularly happy collaboration in 2011 with wildlife and forestry specialists, a hydrologist, a community outreach firm, and a structural engineer. It was a competition for a public space on *St. Patrick's Island* that also housed the Calgary Zoo in Canada. We created a bridge to the island so that wildlife could cross the river, and presented a vibrant assemblage of habitats as an ecological mosaic that will allow local fauna and flora to thrive. This island was designed to become a worldwide model exemplifying a new human attitude toward other species, in contrast to the conventional zoo.

Traditionally, landscape design has been associated with the horizontal plane. Today it resides in vertical green walls of interconnected surface patterning. Do you see green walls and roofs as crossovers into architecture? Are they architecture, or are they landscape? Have the disciplines merged here at the scale of the component?

There has been a break into the vertical plane, it is true. But there is also cave-like work executed below ground, and work above ground perched in the air. Landscape works in other dimensions. The disciplines have not merged, but landscape has invaded architecture's traditional territory, while architecture has invaded landscape's territory in taking on landscape problems.

I don't see the disciplines merging at the level of the component. The component parts of landscape and architecture remain divided above all in one dimension: Landscape deals with living components, as well as engineered components that replicate living ones. Architecture deals with inert materials, although because of landscape and computer programming it is beginning to enter into coding living systems.

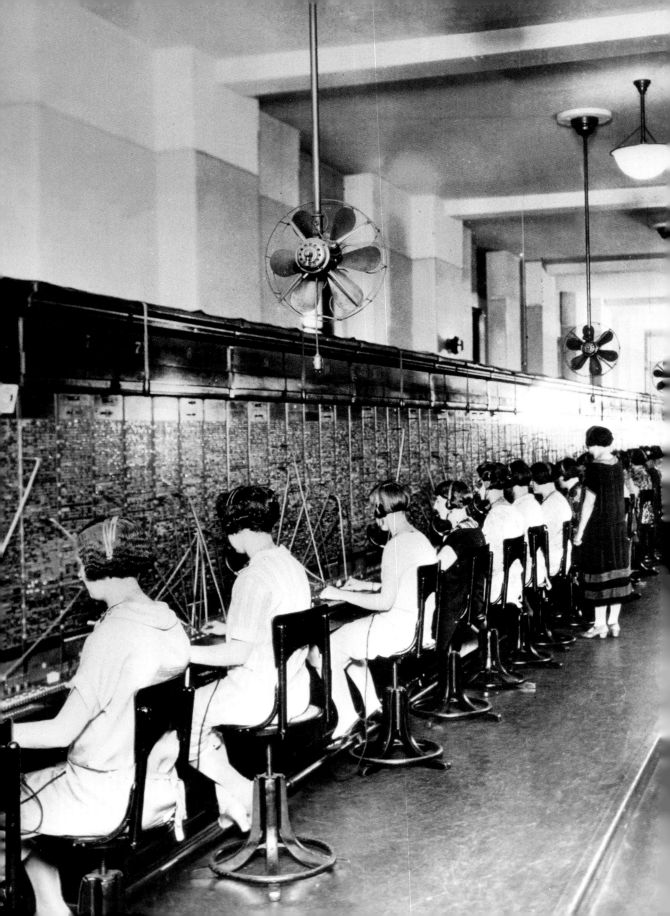

8
Data central

As the use and exchange of building information proliferates, so do the physical requirements needed to house the data. A more recent building typology, known as a "data center", is expected to double in number worldwide within the next two to three years. Such growth represents an evolving design opportunity for the discipline, particularly in regard to BIM. Contrary to popular opinion of "where the internet lives," data-storage buildings are no longer simply utilitarian with anti-monumental status.[1] Instead, the data center has begun to declare its own importance, taking on high-design criteria for inhabitation, strong visible identity, and multiple ideas of performance and scale. In the quest to uncover the depths to which BIM can be applied to design, it is essential to understand the literal buildings that house, among a multitude of data, the information database. What is the relationship between BIM as a new design tool and data centers as a new design problem?

During the early 1990s, when the market demand for better, faster, and exponentially more telecommunication space began to increase, corporations eager to take advantage of newfound high-data bandwidth moved into abandoned buildings that are now commonly referred to as telecommunication, or telco, hotels. This energy infrastructure – essential to powering cell phones – replaced the once spatial and habitable telephone exchange. Just 30 years prior, that typology relied so greatly on human interaction and the space to operate between the private and public spheres of life. The physicality of communication networks at that time provoked patriarchal, gendered associations that came with and contributed to the hierarchy of society. As the data center typology begins to unfold, there are alternative implications to consider in response to demand for information exchange. The more these centers allow for unfettered views into the world of data storage, the more it will impact the future BIM that it supports.

Communications. New York, USA, 1925. Women operating the city's telephone exchange (image provided by Popperfoto and Getty Images)

Pionen White Mountains Data Center, designed by Albert France-Lanord Architects (images provided by Åke E:son Lindman Photography)

Visibility

In general, a data center is a work of immense unseen infrastructure, whose core strategy is organization, whose techniques belong to engineering, and whose fundamental measure is not necessarily that of aesthetic quality. Most people do not care to know where this infrastructure exists or what it looks like, as long as the communication works. Even though data centers are proliferating, they are essentially meant to be undetectable. They typically occupy peripheral locations subject to basic economics of real estate, and the actual buildings often hide in plain sight. But more recently, architects have opted for effective design attention when functional efficiency is critical. The ability to elevate (what might typically result in) standard service infrastructure places an affirmative architectural presence intrinsic to its design. Like a data center, BIM is a repository for data. This brings mechanical BIM to the forefront of architecture BIM. The level of detail and, consequentially, the amount of data needed in a building information model increases even more for digital mechanical infrastructure. The expansion of hosted storage and sharing, increases in download and upload speeds, and the computing force of cloud services will ease concerns about the manageability of large models.[2] As a design platform, BIM offers design teams the sophisticated coordination essential to give the ethereal domain a very real physical presence: above or below ground, outside of or central to urbanization, at various scales, permanent or temporary.

A data center takes on many advantages by concealing itself underground and, in a sense, critiquing the space that a data center makes viable and visible. The *Bahnhof AB Pionen Data Center*, designed by Albert France-Lanord Architects for the independent Swedish internet service provider, is located 30 meters (100 feet) under the granite rocks of the Vita Berg Park in Stockholm. As a Cold War bunker retrofit, the coordination of all necessary parts and pieces – redundant power supplies, data communication connections, environmental controls (e.g., air conditioning, fire suppression), and security devices – is concealed by the massive thickness of stone below ground. At the same time, the design is very much intended to be seen. The lobby space is suspended effortlessly above the sea of data. The minimal glass and steel spaces sit in stark contrast to the rock crypt below – conceptually incorporating a habitable setting for its public market. This covert embedment and Ken Adam-esque sci-fi setting sparks people's imagination of data intrigue for the company that hosted *Wikileaks* through the Edward Snowden crisis. Do the advances in high design of this space, from the carefully considered white data cabinets that contrast the stone, to the boutique furniture, raise the bar on the value of data? Although this typology's visibility does not change the function it so much serves, its design status is actually quite important, as is the case of *Bahnhof*, since these facilities now offer co-location hosting, whereby customers frequently visit the place and work there. This glimpse into the underground world of data storage, be it through YouTube video or as a visiting tour, influences how the design of this typology becomes public domain. What, then, is the value of "designing" these spaces for such infrequent visibility? The perception of virtual information, likewise the future BIM that it supports, would become a more tangible entity and perhaps greater appreciation as a known quantity.

To mitigate issues of visibility and the physical control of infrastructure, a system known as the Data Center Infrastructure Management System (DCIM) arose to adjust the power and cooling capacity and resources of a data center as it sets an "invisible" boundary for IT infrastructure. And just as in the IT world, the BIM facility world offers knowledge and information loss between the design, build, and production/operation phase. To solve this issue, the facility world is using BIM and also extending the workflow by integrating with the IT operators. Dynamic information about the building, such as sensor measurements and control signals from the building systems, can be incorporated within BIM to support analysis of building operation and maintenance.[3]

Citibank Data Center building anatomy – BIM diagram (image provided by ARUP Associates)

Performance

Behind every BIM object, database search, project update, or even Twitter tweet lies a gigantic computing infrastructure, at the heart of which exists massive server farms that collectively account for some 230 million tons of carbon dioxide emissions annually.[4] Performance in recent years has come to denote technological optimization rather than a more assumed association to theatrics.[5] A data center engages both of these concepts to suggest new typological kinships to the data it serves. Here, the facility that houses the data trumps the IT equipment housed within it.

Paradoxically, a data center is expected to be efficient in energy usage and simultaneously extremely energy redundant for emergency

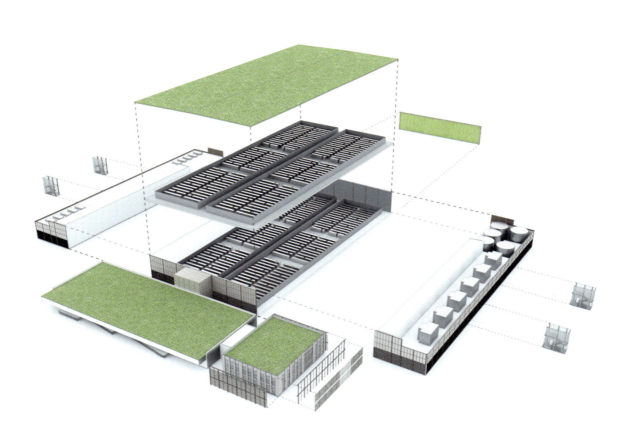

situations or future expansion – so much so that the largest of these facilities use as much electricity as a small town.[6] A data center's power is consumed by two main usages: the energy required to run the actual equipment and that which is required to cool the equipment. Some draw their power from alternative energy fuel cells, while other examples take advantage of geothermal energy for power.[7] In so doing, the data center finds itself acting as a garden. The *Citi Data Center* in Frankfurt, designed by Arup Associates for the American banking corporation Citigroup, Inc., achieves a reduction of energy use for the infrastructure of 72 percent and a reduction of water consumption of 30 percent through design moves that include a green façade surrounding the building.[8] Arup utilized BIM as the means to pass data through design iterations, analysis software, and comparators in order to achieve the best possible results, bearing in mind both measurable and emotive terms. The relationship of BIM to data center is a "new typological kinship" in that, yes, walls and pillars will all be correctly located and power systems can all be modeled for clearances, but more so the BIM system can then ensure that computer room air-conditioning or other cooling systems are positioned correctly in order to provide the right flows to maintain equipment within their thermal limits. Using BIM facilities maintenance also helps to better optimize the energy usage, with excess heat from one part of a building being moved to other areas where heat may be required, or by using heat pumps to offset the amount of energy required to heat water.[9]

Alternatively, performance brings together the theatrics of a concert hall retrofit above (and visible to) a data server hall below. Within an existing 10,000 square meter wood and steel structure built in 1893, the *Bahnhof Gasometer Data Center* (also an Albert France-Lanord Architect design) plays up the views within and beyond to Stockholm's archipelago. A glass floor in the structural addition makes visible the full drama of the building's height and opens to the concert hall experience directly upon entering from below. The original external structure is left entirely untouched and the new programs are accommodated within its loadbearing walls. The path through and around echoes that of a venerated cathedral, moving visitors upward 360° on a floating glass walkway. Moving through the great hall entry, visitors pass the data storage and do not see it again until they are seated spectators within the concert hall. The glass floor of the stage makes data storage visible and ever-present in relation to the theater performance. Spectacular views of the interior roof and beyond contribute to a sense of infinite space above, while the stacks of the data center stand in file as a rational, yet exaggerated, object below. The performance bifurcates at the stage and audience. Is the audience the immediate spectator in the physical theater space or the mass of unseen online users? The stage that was once physically inaccessible to the audience but virtually their domain (through data transferal) 24 hours a day, 7 days a week and 52 weeks a year, now becomes both. Similarly, a multitude of "players" (engineers, fabricators, and now clients) prompt theatricality through infrastructure within a database exchange. The live BIM means authority is granted to those who participate with no lapse in the uptake of information of scenes or who has created them. In addition to producing actual theatricality to match the data center's functionality, the center provides innovative technology for recycling power by selling its excess energy to Sweden's district heating network.[10] These data centers do much more than simply provide the complex service of the internet.

Scale

The *Lefdal Mine Datacenter* is another example that uniquely combines a network of underground tunneling for the purpose of energy performance. Forming the land's edge in the region Sogn og Fjordane, Norway, the mine consists of six stories divided into 75 chambers with a potential white space, or raised floor, area of 120,000 square meters. This data center scales to the point of being more of an urban intervention with "Avenues" and "Streets." CH2M Hill, a global project delivery organization, collaborated with IBM for the initial high-level design, which in the next phase also involved *Lefdal Mine* leaders, local utility companies, end-customers, and other suppliers of hardware. With goals of modularity and scalability, the vast useable floor space allows the design to meet the varying spatial, heating, piping and air-conditioning needs of its tenants. Each floor level consists of a central spiral access road, or data "Avenue," measuring 14 meters wide by 8.5 meters high, suitable for use by two-direction articulated vehicles. The avenue provides direct access to vacant chambers or "streets" on each floor level. Each street varies in depth (averaging 100 meters) but contains part of a four-story concrete building: the data center on the three lower floors and the technical room on the top floor. Such a physical BIM network potentially containing a multitude of BIM content means the data center becomes a recursive urban network.

ON PAGES 192–193
Bahnhof Gasometer Data Center rendering (image provided by Bahnhof, www.bahnhof.net)

Lefdal Mine Datacenter tunnel network scale comparison and detail diagram of a typical avenue (image provided by Lefdal Mine)

The *Lefdal Mine Datacenter* engages ecology as well as urban design. Their energy performance solution is based on the use of cold seawater as a cooling source. Through a heat exchanger, a closed freshwater circuit cools computers via the integrated cold air radiators. The center's proximity to a deep fjord (565 meters) ensures access to unlimited 7.5°C seawater year around. The seawater essentially cools down the freshwater circuit from 30°C to 18°C and enters back into the fjord at 12°C. Experts have verified to the Lefdal Mine company that this will have no impact on the marine life due to the size of the fjord and the tide.[11] As the scale and scope of data centers as a new design problem expands, so will BIM as an infrastructural support system and new design tool.

A data center actually sets in motion (among other things) two interpretations of the term networking – a useful agenda for other typologies. The *Dalles Google Data Center* is set in the picturesque rolling hills of Oregon, it has the right combination of energy infrastructure, developable land, and available workforce to fulfill this perfect storm – meaning the essential data exchange of this vast search engine supplies a connection to nearly 12 billion people per month.[12] The design, led by primary engineers DLB Associates of New Jersey, appears on the exterior to be a typical (but well-polished) industrial factory, whereas the inside contains a colorful network of immense data piping. This demonstrates the instrumental value of the mechanical system that has come to be commonplace, and mostly residual, to the discipline. Such a network requires intense coordination and network of collaboration among many different stakeholders on a project.

An exercise in collaboration for consultants, commonly known as clash detection, tests the integration of several BIM models to compose one master model. Each discipline, including structural engineering, MEP engineering, and environmental engineering, creates a model, independently of all the others, based upon the architect's original model. After each of the disciplines has finished their work, the next step is the process of finding where the elements of separate models occupy the same space, have incompatible parameters or (in 4D BIM modeling) have a time sequence that is out of order. Finding these inconsistencies is vital, as they would severely impact the construction process, causing delays, design changes, material costs, and a cascade of headaches and budget overruns.

The relationship of DLB to a design project represents the changing, multi-dimensional dynamics and outcomes produced when

Google Data Center interior (image provided by Connie Zhou)

incorporating BIM. For the project *Dalles Google*, 4D visualizations provided exactly how the construction progress would occur and optimized the sequencing of the expansive network of piping. Early recognition of any potential challenges was also mitigated by a 5D model database of cost control and distribution to all project participants. Such availability of quantity takeoffs led to more accurate bids and fewer change orders. A 6D BIM took the model beyond the completion of the construction phase to become an integral part of the intelligent data-driven operation of the built facility. In this instance, the BIM becomes a lifetime virtual graphical navigation tool and central container of facility design. Construction and operational information is used to further analyze and test operation efficiency and energy savings.

The color-coded mechanical system of *Dalles Google* scales to its virtual capacity, while providing distinguishable clarity for those who service it. Hot water pipe is red, while cold water is blue. In the context of its infrastructural approach, the display of such synchronized mechanical systems demonstrates a new dexterity of collaboration in terms of mechanical integration. Like a tightly organized laboratory, this center celebrates and engenders a fresh, festive environment for only 150 employees, similar to the colorful logo on its webpage and the exposed innards of the *Centre Pompidou*. *Dalles* holds true what Andrew Blum so poignantly points out as the space that houses the "mirror of our identities, the physical embodiment of our most personal facts and feelings."[13] Varying the relationship of participant to data house and the degree of its inhabitation, a normative BIM exercise is elevated into the interior event that far exceeds its program. It is hard to imagine this type of hyper-synthesized interior existing without the use of BIM or its process of collaboration.

Conclusion

A data center design provides a clear commentary on prevailing architectural issues of our time: an equivocation between functional and visual sides of architecture, engaging in the former while ever extolling the latter, respecting if not valorizing the primacy of the actual building. The advances of information modeling make possible the physicality of such by-product urban space, which in the end makes the data center more central to its locale of necessity, concurrently combining a public with a private program.

These centers offer a physical outcome for human interaction and engagement with communication and information exchange. Reciprocally, perhaps no other project type stands to benefit more from the level of coordination made possible by building information modeling and virtual design and construction than the data center. What alternative types of performance can we expect to see the data center embrace in the future? Returning to the space of the telephone operators, value is being placed on the occupancy or visibility of the data center. In this sense, the correlation of design to mechanical systems brought on by the organization of BIM is profound and generative in its overarching use of clash detection. This data house unveils a world of hidden BIM – a world of the infrastructural "elsewhere" that could be a discussion of a new speculative design plateau. It is now inspirational to ask: "Do you know where your data lives?"

Notes

1. Andrew Blum, *Tubes: A Journey to the Center of the Internet* (New York, NY: HarperCollins Publishers, 2013).
2. Sam Robins, "The Future of BIM," *HPAC Engineering*, April 23, 2013, http://hpac.com/archive/future-bim (retrieved December 14, 2014).
3. http://infrarati.wordpress.com/2013/06/19/datacenters-blending-bim-dcim-cmdb-etc/ (retrieved December 14, 2014).
4. www.onearth.org/article/how-cool-is-tha (retrieved August 22, 2014).
5. Kryygiel, Eddy. "Using Building Information Modeling for Performance-Based Design," *Fabricating Architecture*, ed. Robert Corser (New York, NY: Princeton Architectural Press, 2010).
6. James Glanz, "Power, Pollution and the Internet," *New York Times*, September 22, 2012, www.nytimes.com/2012/09/23/technology/data-centers-waste-vast-amounts-of-energy-belying-industry-image.html (retrieved July 15, 2014).
7. James Glanz, "eBay Plans Data Center That Will Run on Alternative Energy Fuel Cells," *New York Times*, June 20, 2012, www.nytimes.com/2012/06/21/technology/ebay-plans-data-center-that-will-use-alternative-energy.html (retrieved July 13, 2014).
8. The Frankfurt Centre will use only 30 percent of the power required for services that a conventional data center would utilize and only 40 percent of the heating energy. This results in an overall annual CO_2 emission reduction of 11,750 tons. Cooling water consumption is also a major factor in this type of building and, through the use of innovative reverse osmosis water treatment in the cooling plant, Arup Associates' design saves 35,950,000 liters per annum.
9. www.computerweekly.com/feature/Combining-DCIM-and-BIM-tools-for-effective-datacentre-management (retrieved December 27, 2014).
10. Penny Jones, "Bahnhof Takes Data Center Design to New Level," *Datacenter Dynamics,* March 19, 2013, www.datacenterdynamics.com/focus/archive/2013/03/bahnhof-takes-data-center-design-new-level (retrieved August 20, 2014).
11. "Cooling," *Lefdal Mine*, www.lefdalmine.com/cooling (retrieved August 15, 2014).
12. Craig Smith, "By the Numbers: 60 Amazing Google Search Statistics and Facts," *Digital Market Ramblings*, October 28, 2014, http://expandedramblings.com/index.php/by-the-numbers-a-gigantic-list-of-google-stats-and-facts/#.U5tGGSiqQqg (retrieved August 22, 2014).
13. Blum, *Tubes*, pp. 229.

Bibliography
Alger, Douglas, *The Art of the Data Center: A Look Inside the World's Most Innovative and Compelling Computing Environments.* 1st edition. Upper Saddle River, NJ: Prentice Hall, 2012.
Varnelis, Kazys, "The Centripetal City: Telecommunications, the Internet, and the Shaping of the Modern Urban Environment," *Cabinet Magazine* 17 (spring 2004/2005).

[INTERVIEW]

Marc Fornes
THEVERYMANY

At the 2011 TEX-FAB in San Antonio, Texas, your keynote address referred to one of your installation pieces as an information model, specifically to the annotation that coincided the multiple components in its assemblage. How do you define an information model (or is this the extent of BIM to you)? And how does it enable your design process and expectations of output?

I think that talk came as a reaction to my 1990s generation workflow, where everything was texture mapped or made to be a rendering because actually not much of that work was going to construction. Because we didn't want those ideas to just disappear as a lot of 1960s and 1970s era work did, we started to replace every single element by computing pixel into actual geometry. In other words, image became geometry. The challenges of assembly in terms of time consumption, logistics, and team management reminded us of a workflow when an architect produced as few production files as possible and produced construction documents themselves. We wanted our 3D file to actually fabricate the project or its machining parts. If something were to go wrong, we would pay for it in the end because it wouldn't reassemble. So we went from pixel to trying to place as much information as possible into our model so that every single tab, hole, number, etc. was accountable and then physically produced. The file size made this approach unmanageable. We realized that the only reason we actually need to transfer into geometry is to reread the level of intelligence of our 3D model for the physical world. That's when we decided a lot of things we were going to do would be only information – sets of coordinates, order of coordinates, lists of those elements, number of connectors, and also what the name is, of itself, but also of its neighbors. A complex part or surface would run agents without geometry. They only become geometry once you want to actually physically produce and unroll them. And that's where in the lecture I probably talk about agent-centric modeling. If you already

Willow detail, Borden Park, Edmonton Arts Council, Edmonton, Canada (image courtesy of Doyle C. Marko/ DCMPhotography.ca)

know attributes for every part, the environment around it, and the number of its right or left part, that's actually information modeling or management which enables it to reassemble faster. We want to be able to assemble these projects that have 80,000 unique parts, and to make those different layers of information available by physically engraving it and physically translating it so that anyone can use it.

In writing a chapter on data centers, I found a striking resemblance of the synchronized mechanical systems in the Google Data Center to your earlier research called Adaptive Clips, which suggested a system of "clips" onto a primary set of non-uniform longitudinal structural members. Do you foresee physical data connections as part of a future of this exploration with computational weaving of systems, infrastructural perchance?

It's a good question and a funny correlation. The weaving, at least at the time of the bridge, actually came from that understanding of computation as a very serial set of protocols. BIM always begins with an interface, but behind is just sets of code. It just reads it in a very linear way. A lot of things run into the matrix which is storing information into a number of columns and number of lines. Every cell has a depth and eventually within that cell you have several other alternative dimensions. Architecture is 99 percent 2D, a lot 3D, and then computation is actually N sets of dimensions. The best way to visualize it, I think, is to imagine searching for a file in a file cabinet. In that cabinet, there are a number of files. That's one dimension. If I am looking for file number 3, line number 5. That's already three dimensions (where architects typically stop). Then you say in that file number 3, I need a specific sheet of paper in the folder (fourth dimension) or read me the first line (fifth dimension) and then just read me the first word (sixth dimension) and tell me the third letter (seventh dimension). Tell me if it is a sans serif character or not, etc. That's dimension. The bridge was just that – a physical manifestation of the way we store information. At that stage in our type of production, I did not look into ways to manifest the Nth dimension of storage in 3D or in the building environment.

I am interested in the conceptual framework that can shift our understanding of production in the physical environment. My three-year-old daughter already knows more about an iPad than my parents, and probably in two years' time will get a 3D printer for Christmas to print her own toys. That generation will understand dimension in a way that we do not necessarily grasp at that stage. The generation just behind me understands an "apps-related model" and trust that information is somewhere, out there in the cloud. To some extent, they do not really understand or care exactly what a server is or which server their data comes from or who owns that server. Yes, we all know how to download and install apps and use them, but more importantly the actual concept of thinking is no longer localized to a desktop. It's the same type of shift, I think, of our understanding of geometry of three dimensions versus N dimensions of computation.

In your larger projects, how has BIM been beneficial or detrimental in terms of collaboration?

At the end of the day, I think everything is driven by time and a contract, and that's what I respect most about the BIM industry – that it is trying to push a type of contract and the type of liability. But what doesn't work currently is the sequential aspect of BIM. It is never happening simultaneously across the board. The guy modeling the concrete aspect for the Louis Vuitton Paris Museum and the guy modeling the façade hardly talk to each other. So the clash between those entities is still huge, yet it is probably going to be the building that advertises the most use of BIM ever. I'm actually very critical of what we've experienced with the growth in scale of our work. We are literally riding out that issue on the *Chrysalis Amphitheater* project, which is largely a collaboration with ARUP. When we only have a certain amount of weeks on the project and they say they are not going to start working until after our design is done, there is actually no computation or collaboration taking place. There is no BIM. It is a missed opportunity as they are one of the largest engineering firms that definitely advertises the use of BIM technology and we are known for use of computation. I think BIM allows some to pretend that everything is parametric and in effect adaptable, but this is a complete fallacy of parametricism. The discipline really needs what I call a "search" model – one that allows collaborators to write rules and establish a system that can find and adapt within the time frame of the design. It is not just a smarter representation heavy with attributes, which BIM is kind of becoming, but instead using the computation to give endless amounts of variation in an instant. In many instances, a BIM is a way to increase fees because somehow the client thinks the product is better because everything gets modeled. But the data center, as you mentioned, of the organization of information is not even touching the BIM and the BIM is barely touching the mass of architecture. SHoP is probably the one firm who are doing BIM in parallel through their construction and design studio setup. The sequential setup either slows down the designer or slows down the mechanical engineer.

Willow detail, Borden Park, Edmonton Arts Council, Edmonton, Canada (image courtesy of Doyle C. Marko/DCMPhotography.ca)

Has your process of design through code shifted for the building scale?

Not with the scale. We just finished a project called *Willow Dome* in Edmonton, Canada which is the first full-scale, permanent structure where everything went smoothly. It is in a park so there is no institution to control or change it and, being outdoors, we had to deal with snow and wind loads. We produced the fabrication files for the machining parts, but another company is assembling it. And the next one is an amphitheater in France which is about twice the scale of the Edmonton project. We are at a stage where we have quite a few projects in the office and the Edmonton one is the type of process we hope to build upon. We used color for each piece as an attribute. It is completely self-supported with no primary structure and assembled with larger aluminum rivets. We have a bridge project that still falls under public art, but we tried to bring program into the shape, not to just grow in scale in order to be a larger piece, but to also transform its use and function. And then we have another that is literally 100 feet wide and that's probably the point where we face issues of constructability. But as was mentioned, it comes down to client and contractual relations. That's what is unfortunate for us, that the largest project we have ever is facing so many issues. But the issues have nothing to do with scale.

There is evidence for BIM to extend into a post-construction role of facilities management or maintenance. To what extent do you see a database extending beyond the life of its outcome?

We are having a similar but different type of situation with institutions. When they collect a piece, they want the data files

behind it as well. The *Y/Surf/Struc* at the Centre Pompidou in Paris, for example, is a permanent piece on display in their collection. Because they started collecting early digital art, many of those files cannot be run or operate anymore because the data storage devices are outdated and such. Institutions already have trouble even opening a file, much less dealing with storage of its future. To maintain that file or file type for operability or even have someone on staff who understands the knowledge of the organization of the file is an issue. For a model to eventually grow and adapt for indexing into a new model is a complex challenge. I think developers have an interest in this side of BIM, but I have yet to see a true example of the design execution model become the operative control model for maintaining a building.

Willow detail, Borden Park, Edmonton Arts Council, Edmonton, Canada (image courtesy of Doyle C. Marko/DCMPhotography.ca)

Are there other conditions of data inquiry or collaborations well outside of our typical play group (i.e., structural and mechanical engineers) that you have intentions to develop in the future?

We are less interested in the conceptual collaborations, like working with a biologist or material scientist to understand their innovation. Yes, their work is intriguing, but I am more interested specifically in the use of technology today, not 5–20 years from now. I'm more into collaborations with similar mindsets using technology driven for customization and performance, rather than by its cheapest solution. Obviously performance leads to economics, but the priority is for efficiency.

Is building the ultimate goal or will there always be a side to your research that tends to more experimentation at a smaller scale?

I said it ten years ago, and I maintain the position: we want to build. Whatever we do, it needs to be scalable. If it is not scalable it is a failure. And we market a lot of failures in the sense that even if the system is apparently stable and visually pleasing. If the assembly takes too long, it cannot grow in scale and eventually cannot raise the construction industry. But at the same time, I am realistic to know that we need a minimum of at least one project in every scale in order to eventually build a tower. So we are trying to grow carefully in scale with the end goal definitely in the building.

ON PAGES 208–209
Willow view in the winter, Borden Park, Edmonton Arts Council, Edmonton, Canada (image courtesy of Doyle C. Marko/DCMPhotography.ca)

9

bigBIM

BIM, with its potential to expand and impact the discipline, seems intrinsically related to the influence of another highly touted cultural force: big data. Simply defined as the accumulation of knowledge, big data amasses and tracks information, then recycles and recombines it into usable formats. Scientists, pharmaceutical companies, and financial analysts, to name a few highly visible groups, have long used large data sets to answer complex questions, frequently to their great financial advantage. Business analyst Michael Hasler actually views data as a highly valued commodity, referring to it as the "new oil." For architecture, big data could solve any number of issues – be it culture values or communal efforts of a project discussed in earlier chapters. If BIM has truly produced the reputed paradigm shift in architecture, how can the process be inclusive of and as all-encompassing as big data? Just how "big" is BIM currently, and how much bigger could it come to be? The well-known "Four V's" of big data – "volume, velocity, variety, and veracity" – show potential to be harnessed in this process. Similarly, BIM has a capacity to produce big data of its own in ways that have yet to be found or explored.

In the end, who controls an autonomous BIM, as it gets bigger and controls more aspects of the built environment? The individual user, the client who commissioned it, or a greater public entity involved in the empirically grounded quest for truth *writ large*? Government, state power, or local planning departments are electing to adopt (and in some cases enforce) information-rich BIM technology as a form of fact finding and implementation.[1] The idea that this process of control and collaborative behavior will unlock new and more efficient ways of working means that at all stages of a project life cycle, from the local to the global scale, exchange is active and thus developing BIM into something bigger than itself. As information models become more central to the operation of buildings, the capacity for BIM to serve an important managerial role raises questions over whether this transformation will become more of an inhibitor or provocateur to architectural design.

Plot visualization by time of day per 289 users from Tel Aviv over three months (image courtesy of Nadav Hochman, Lev Manovich, Jay Chow – Phototrails.net)

COLUMBARIUM HABITABILE

The Inhabited Columbarium or the reservation for old little houses and their inhabitants in a large modern city.

A House dies twice: the first time when people leave it, then it can be saved if they return; the second time finally when it is destroyed. In some cities where the modern subletting of most pushed old buildings, there are still a number of old little houses with people living there for many years, till these houses must be destroyed according to a general city plan and people living in them must receive flats in new buildings. There is only one possibility for the owner of such a house to save it: let there take 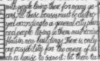 be the house from its place and put it into a Columbarium — a huge concrete cake standing in the centre of the city. But they do not only of the owner and his family continue living in their house not standing on a shelf in a con- crete box. While they live in it, the house lives also, but if they can not live in these conditions anymore and refuse, their house is destroyed and its place becomes empty waiting for the next one.

Brodsky & Utkin's *Columbarium Habitabile*, 1989–1990, projects portfolio, 1981–1990, 43 × 31¾ inches (photo credit: D. James Dee, image courtesy of Ronald Feldman Fine Arts, New York)

BIM collective

To speculate the potential of a bigger BIM, the life of a small BIM does not end when construction is complete or even when the owner occupies the building. The copperplate etching *Columbarium Habitabile* by Alexander Brodsky and Ilya Utkin visualizes a collective life of nostalgic house-like models sitting within an expansive hypothetical gridded framework. The columbarium, meant to signify 1960s high-rise blocks, and its mysteriously hung wrecking ball suggests that "a house dies twice" – the first time when people leave it, and the second time when it is destroyed. Similarly, a BIM model holds the potential for two lives, but conversely a life lived twice – initially as a design model, and then as a continuous and seamless archive sitting within a framework for sharing building data between stakeholders, owners, disciplines, and a variety of applications. In this speculation, the BIM collective, once shelved with other post-construction BIMs, lives on autonomously and more importantly serves as the mechanism to maintain a building over any or all phases of its lifecycle. Much more than a mere 3D database existing solely for design and construction information, BIM has the potential capability of extending representation into reality.

A networked grid, like the columbarium, exists today, but alternatively in the form of virtual modeled space of big data – one which BIM engages and expands. Web sources, like the "National BIM Library," act as repositories for open-source BIM data sets, object files, and information to then generate a stock of ideas for building. Designers can use such websites and vast data content to improve their design through the breadth of choices and dissemination of better decisions. Government agencies are also gaining a foothold in the analytical understanding of how BIM, as a required aspect of every project submission, will allow the architectural discipline (along with those outside of it) to leverage a wider array of data. These tasks expand BIM into a critical state of collaboration between designers, consultants, and other stakeholders in order to maximize its potential – engaging constituents from both local and global positions.[2] To better understand the scalability of BIM, this may mean stepping outside of conventional agencies of design and reconsidering fully what a BIM really is.

New plateaus

Large data sets, when analyzed in tandem with other information, can reveal patterns and relationships that would otherwise remain hidden. Much depends upon how the data are processed, or the context in which they are viewed. Data scientist and researcher Niall Gafney observes with regard to the Hubble Space Telescope's Ultra Deep Field probing: "What you can get out of data is endless, but the exact same data can either be used to solve the behavior of a galaxy or alternatively as an image for a Hallmark card."[3] Like the data collection of Hubble's distant universe, the domain of BIM is increasing beyond the building into many scales and plateaus, meaning BIM is being implemented as an expansive network of projects on ground, below ground for infrastructure, and well above in the virtual computing cloud. Such divergent and global BIM contexts hold potential for pursuit of answers to the "unknown unknowns," by translating information to and from an architectural model and its life cycle.

To help locate and record concealed assets, the City of Las Vegas, led by the engineering, planning, and surveying firm VTN Consulting, have fully modeled underground BIM infrastructure. The project resulted in an extensive amount of data geometry that becomes visible on-site through hardware viewers (like an iPad) running the Android platform. Above ground, a global scale 3D urban and landscape geometry network, known as City Geography Markup Language (CityGML), has been adopted as a common information model that defines classes and relationships for the most relevant topographic objects. In city and regional models, with respect to their geometrical, topological, and appearance properties, CityGML defines everything from site buildings, bridges, and tunnels to even city furniture and natural features. Such geometry-rich, graphic content can produce sophisticated BIM for different domains of analysis, including simulations, urban data mining, and facility management.[4]

Global governing bodies, such as the Building and Construction Authority of Seoul or the General Services Administration Initiative of the United States, are reinforcing the proliferation of small BIM. By working in conjunction with industry, their efforts underpin broader control of development in order to help reduce capital costs and decrease the carbon footprint that results from construction and building operations.[5] The United Kingdom Government Cabinet Office announced their Construction Strategy intention to require

City of Las Vegas BIM infrastructure (image provided by VTN Consulting)

a collaborative 3D BIM for all projects, asset information, and documentation by 2016.[6] Other countries, such as India, are approaching BIM primarily as a means to boost their economy by acting as a modeling service to companies abroad.[7] Municipal agencies, like the New York City Department of Design + Construction, offer "BIM Guidelines" that require its use, and go so far as to even specify detail, object type, and mandatory parameters.[8] In this regard, BIM extends into the workflows, content, and documentation of many design stakeholders within the global context of building and planning.

Sydney Opera House BIM (image/photo courtesy of Sydney Opera House and Johnson Pilton Walker)

Management

Within the BIM acronym, the term "modeling" is often replaced in a derogatory manner with the word "management." Rather than a perception of management through BIM as a design liability, designers can indeed benefit from the platform's ability to organize and help maintain more complex and sophisticated architecture. The daily operations of the *Sydney Opera House* provide an impressive example of facilities management using a post-construction BIM. The iconic and unique curved shells designed by Jørn Utzon in 1973 contain seven theatres, 37 plant rooms, 12 elevators, and more than 1,000 other complex program spaces. The facility has since been updated through BIM collaboration between Utzon Architects, Johnson Pilton Walker, and Arup to optimize its accommodations for 300 full-time and 500–600 part-time staff members for some 1,500 performances and 1,000 other events it hosts each year. The Australian government, together with the Facility Management Association of Australia (FMA Australia), selected this UNESCO World Heritage building to explore a comprehensive BIM support system for all of the asset and facility management operations required on a day-to-day basis.[9] Mundane activities, such as turning off lights at an appointed hour, give vital functionality for facilities management (FM), but speculatively BIM will be programmed to play more of a role in the theatrical performances. This level of sophisticated BIM also goes back to the question of authority: who controls the model before and after a project's completion, and is FM now part of schematic design?

For new construction, what might the future of FM hold for a more day-to-day typology, such as a supermarket? Self-checkout stations already exist in many large stores, putting a new spin on convenience

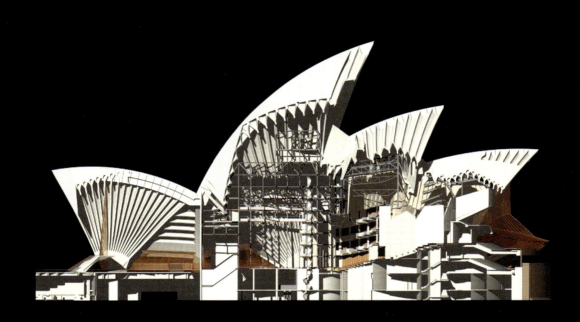

and at-will virtual management. For the UK-based *Tesco Store in Sheringham*, Pinnacle Construction inherited a design from Wilkinson Eyre Architects, one of the UK's leading architectural practices, based in London, England. The project relied greatly on BIM technology to execute the complex timber roof structure, an unusual design deliverable for a supermarket. But more so, efforts to ease the transfer and translation of information between managing disciplines in real time allowed for a high level of precision and coordination, so much so, the BIM and final outcome are close to identical.[10] How similar to the real-world experience is the simulated BIM, and is this simulation creating redundancy of the virtual database to the real world?

Perhaps more significantly, model-sharing leads to advanced forms of simulation. This visualization creates a complete virtual shopping experience for the client to analyze during the design phase. This speaks to an innovative level of preconstruction control and evaluation that can then equally unfold in post-construction management capabilities and thus the experience of a building. Hypothetically, a BIM will begin to maintain the physical store as much as the virtual "aisles" that let people buy groceries via their smartphones, whereby each item (with its corresponding QR code) is scanned in a store app, items are "checked out" from a virtual shopping cart, and then get delivered right to a user's doorstep.[11] A speculative BIM "store manager" would know instantly which items needed to be restocked, which have sold the most in any given day or time, and which have been misplaced in the physical store.

When presented with the potential scale of a virtual construct that maintains and manages the real world, architects have the dramatic opportunity to design and work beyond the construction documents phase. Instead, they are charged with developing the next phase of a BIM that would connect to the real world, in which design really becomes part of the experiential environment. Facilities management is just a step in that direction that, as Greg Lynn put it, "is somewhat not that interesting in its current usage."[12] A BIM of multiplicity or scaled to that of an entire city is when the paradigm shift will truly occur. The possibilities, big or small, of what that life cycle holds for the future of design are dramatic.

Analyzing

Modeling tools have grown increasingly complex – in architecture as in other fields – with the increase in data-intensity of corresponding

Tesco Stores Ltd. Supermarket in Sheringham, BIM rendering versus reality (all images © Tekla Corporation and Pinnacle Consulting Engineers Limited)

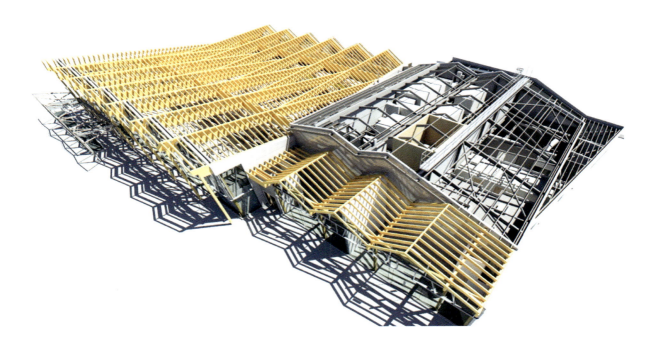

file size, storage, and management. In response, collaboration between design team members has also become much more involved by technologies such as web-based 3D collaboration, cloud-based data management, and infrastructure-as-a-service. These features are said to improve communication and enhance a team's ability to analyze situations before, during, and after they occur. As BIM parallels the rise of "big data," be it cultural monitoring or just the mere size of a project, firms scale their technical capacity on demand and utilize the rapid deployment of additional computing nodes.

Best known for highly customized, titanium building envelopes, Frank Gehry and Partners believes opportunities for BIM *writ large* will come out of the collaborative nature of software. The data structure of the *Fondation Louis Vuitton Museum*, which opened outside of Paris in 2014, is the pinnacle of multiple user development for their office to date. As such, the project is a catalyst for rethinking the roles and control over the design process. In true Gehry fashion, the form appears to deny gravity and any standard tropes of architecture, even his own. Differing from past Gehry projects, the building allows its visitors to occupy the *poché* space and conveys a tectonic proclivity of exposed and celebrated details. According to Dennis Sheldon, a founder and Chief Technology Officer of Gehry Technologies, "at any given time in the design phase there were 200 people working on the model around the world with extraordinary parametric knowledge – all embedding and creating intelligent objects."[13] Did this intensive and extensive BIM production change the execution of Gehry's very particular design process or just make it easier to resolve? Greater recognition of the parts and pieces that support such challenging geometry appear to be accommodated, and more so celebrated.

Data transmission can be mapped and controlled through evolving networks of information, both locally and globally, or through what is referred to as "the cloud." There are two views of the cloud. One is that it's just a different way of delivering updates to software, and the other is that it allows for connected information. The latter concept of cloud content management – that based on connectivity – underpins the belief that new data storage services allow for innovative design practices. Tracking design changes and their details is part and parcel of the responses to them. On one level, the hierarchy of BIM defines the control, but the system can support different versions of control and can be implemented into the setup of a project; specifying who is allowed to transmit and

Fondation Louis Vuitton Museum data structure (photo credit to Vincent Capman, Paris Match Collection, Getty Images)

have access to the organization. Transparency and accessibility of the data is critical, as it can no longer hide in a lost paper trail.

The *Fondation Louis Vuitton Museum* will most likely be award-winning for its quality of space and form, but should more so be recognized for its innovation of instantaneous access to information globally and simultaneously across all BIM files. The *Vuitton Museum* is extraordinarily removed from the way the industry has been structured in the past. Typically, free-flowing creative activity happens in every silo (architects, engineers, etc.) of a design process, and due to the limitations of translation there is very little cross-over between these different silos. Creativity also tended to be compressed into a very rarefied way of communicating: 2D documentation. The *Vuitton Museum* demonstrates control and responsibility through BIM, not the 2D documents of very specific points in the design process, and is said to have allowed transactions to happen much faster than those in the standard phase of design development. According to Sheldon,

> Communication and collaboration occurred much more frequently, and the model evolved into an associated state of multiple inputs. The result was an expanded network of BIM objects and revisions and ancillary information of who did it, what was their intentions, and why. So there is this explosion of integrated BIM data in conjunction with all the kinds of collaborative mechanisms that happen around it.[14]

The approach on this project now sets a standard for how updates and organization by discipline (or by floor or sub-discipline or room) can be handled. Management and design changes acknowledge a level of distributive BIM sophistication that has led to innovation in the data structure itself. BIM, in this instance, creates a direct connection between the value of information and the value of the decision makers in the supply chain (i.e., architects, owners, and makers), whereby a small BIM using big data turns a scenario into big BIM.

Fondation Louis Vuitton Museum data structure (image courtesy of Dennis Sheldon, Gehry Technology)

Conclusion

In the 1950s, environmentalists Eugene and Howard Odum introduced the concept of an ecosystem to the scientific discipline that was previously only focused on individualized, small-scale studies. In the

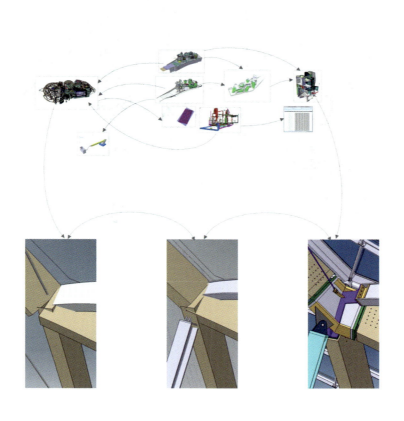
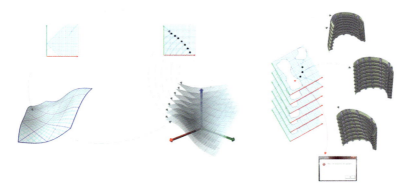

same manner, the inclusion of data in the discipline of architecture creates a broader "ecology" of design. The concept of "big data" extends the scope and generality it encompasses to the design discipline by recognizing, including, and classifying large entities – even those at the scale of the world – thereby offering up the sense that being "big" gives BIM an infinite scale and applicability. The question, then, is one of information consumption: whether too much information at this stage could potentially congest the design process. And it is uncertain whether BIM can provide a pervasive "big" database for a discipline where many firms are still struggling to merely traverse the workflow and complexities of a simple or small BIM database. A wealth of data does not necessarily equate to or guarantee a wealth of design information.

Big data is not just a visualization, but an actuality. It takes the form of the most complex discipline-related collaborations from cost values to geopolitical video data from Facebook, or more specifically feedback reports from the field – reports like those produced by CASE, a New York BIM consultant firm – that recycle and recombine BIM construction. By producing performance analysis based on day-to-day on-site observation, BIM turns building production into a usable record with the potential to capture and centralize data for building efficiency.[15] Does big data translate into more capital, better design, or, better yet, more altruistic pursuits? When projects that fit the small data/small BIM category already require many layers of complex design process, would big data just mean a bigger disruption or the transformational change the discipline really needs? If data beyond the building are never used or even gathered in the first place, the discipline stands to witness the wrecking ball of Brodsky and Utkin. BIM, and its enhanced potential through big data, offers a hopeful, almost utopian perspective on the future of this technology.

Notes
1. BIM is called a rich model because all objects in it have properties and relationships, and this information can be used for data mining to develop simulations or calculations using the model data. An example is the ability to perform automated code checking to confirm egress, fire ratings, or thermal load calculations.
2. As a way of incorporating big data into BIM, this chapter relies on the structure used to frame big data in biotechnology, as put forward by Sophien Kamoun and Daniel MacLean, "Big Data in Small Places," *Nature Biotechnology* 30.1 (January 2012): 33.
3. Niall Gaffney, "Diving into Data: Harnessing the Power of Information," presentation delivered at the University of Texas, AT&T Executive Education and Conference Center, March 4, 2014.

4   "CityGML: City Geography Markup Language," *CityGMLwiki.org*, July 2, 2013, www.citygmlwiki.org/index.php/Main_Page (retrieved May 12, 2014).
5   Lachmi Khemlani, "Around the World with BIM," *AECbytes.com*, May 9, 2012, http://aecbytes.com/feature/2012/Global-BIM.html (retrieved June 21, 2014).
6   Report published by the UK Cabinet Office on May 31, 2011.
7   J. Vinoth Kumar and Mahua Mukherjee, "Scope of Building Information modeling (BIM) in India," *Journal of Engineering Science and Technology Review* 2 (December 2009).
8   New York City/Department of Design + Construction, *BIM Guidelines Part Three Submission and Deliverables* (July 2012), p. 21.
9   *Adopting BIM for Facilities Management: Solutions for Managing the Sydney Opera House* (Sydney: Cooperative Research Centre for Construction Innovation, 2007). This publication is an abridged version of the FM Exemplar Project's Digital Modeling Report, the compilation of which was led by John Mitchell (consultant to CSIRO).
10 The stakeholders combined multiple 3D models featuring steel, timber, and reinforced concrete, and shared these models between all parties.
11 Torben Rick, "Will Virtual Stores Disrupt Traditional Bricks and Mortar," *Torbenrick.eu*, May 23, 2013, http://www.torbenrick.eu/blog/strategy/will-virtual-stores-disrupt-traditional-retail/.
12 Greg Lynn, interview with the author, September 25, 2014.
13 Dennis Sheldon, interview with the author, May 21, 2014. Since this interview, Gehry Technologies was bought by the American technology firm Trimble.
14 Ibid.
15 Cominetti, Matteo, and Tyler Goss, "Performance Analytics: A No-Hype Introduction to Big Data for Architecture, Engineering, and Construction," presentation delivered at Autodesk University, Las Vegas, Nevada, December 4, 2014.

[INTERVIEW]

Christopher Sharples and John Cerone
SHOP ARCHITECTS

Standard BIM techniques have gained the reputation of being simply a directive toward documentation, and to some extent engendering a more restrained approach to architectural design. How has BIM enabled SHoP's design process and expectations of output to rise above this tendency?

Sharples: I think it's important to relay that when we got out of school in the early 1990s, we were all coming from different backgrounds, from business to fine arts to engineering. After getting our master's degrees in architecture, we made the casual or naive assumption that whatever we design, anyone could just build it. As a solution, we thought to work through models, and that was at a time when new software enabled us to not only build physical models, but to develop the digital ones as well. So from very early on, we began managing very complex information of a building through a 3D model, instead of standard 2D or section drawings. We also started to rethink or re-choreograph the way we shared information from a representational approach to a directive for construction instead. We felt very confident as designers, but wanted to also have capability in translating our designs into buildings. A design model is not necessarily useful to a builder and we realized that we were doing a lot of extra work during the construction document phase and through construction administration, especially when we were generating models and fabrication information for the contractor and the subs. We thought to start that process much earlier on would allow for better control of the cost and would also influence the way we design. John and his team are now really focused on how you take that design model and translate it.

Cerone: SHoP's Virtual Design and Construction division is relatively new but is recognized as a scope of the practice that is working off these coat-tails of BIM.

Konza Techno City master plan (image courtesy of SHoP Architects PC, 2014)

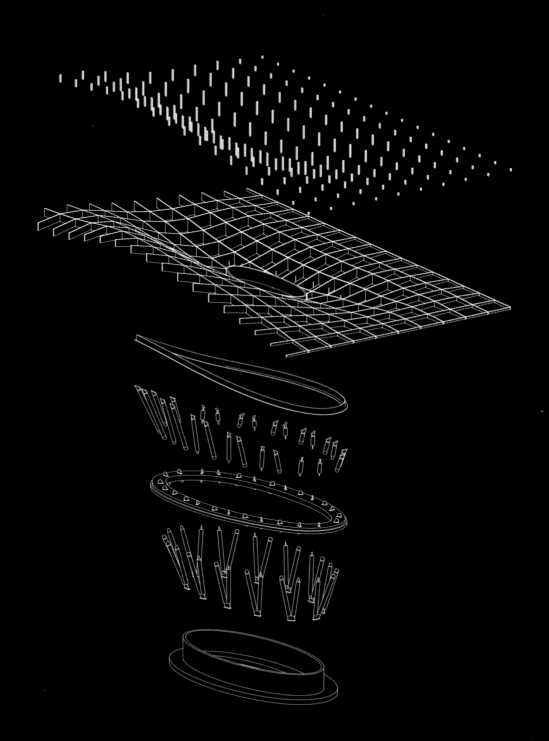

Konza Techno Hub BIM detailing (image courtesy of SHoP Architects PC, 2014)

John, are you and your team involved in the design process from day one?

Cerone: Yes, the office aims for the ideal situation on a project which is where the systems applications are happening parallel to the design. The BIM technology is allowing us to best align that process.

Sharples: The fact is, a lot of projects die or don't move forward because of issues of cost, complexity, and time added to manage it all. The idea is that we can think about issues, such as material take-off or 4D of time and 5D of cost management, very early in the design process to help alleviate any surprises that might cause a project to stop.

How does SHoP view planning departments' required BIM submission? Is it a hindrance (meaning too much government control/involvement) or an enabler for better organizing standards across the discipline?

Sharples: We take it very seriously and are happy when such requirements exist. A key factor is that the requirement be part of the design process, but the big disconnect is when a builder goes to construction and they usually don't use that model. They either want the output in 2D traditional documents or they want to rebuild the model themselves. So there is a lot of design information and time lost as a result of that situation. When we go into these conversations, it is important to have the client or government agency understand that the model is part of an iterative process. The model changes as various inputs get updated, whether it's a design program input or a constructability cost input, and these factors greatly influence the model. It tracks all the way through the entire process, so at the very end you have made an as-built model that is holding or is engrained with all these data that can be useful for building. These agencies could maintain a BIM and it could be more of an open architecture where the building actually gets better with time because the model can be updated.

Would you say that BIM cloud content management or external storage service promotes reliability and security of design?

Cerone: It definitely helps with efficiency and any efficiency helps secure the design. Our technical workflow and collaborative models and data are preferably stored in one central location where everyone is accessing real-time information. For example, we are often involved directly with fabricators and they are pulling the necessary information directly from our models, so in that sense the idea that the model is a real-time understanding of the information that we are outputting and that they are extracting assures better quality of the built outcome.

    Sharples: And having devices that are robust enough to allow us to go into the field with those models to communicate directly (as was the case with *Barclays*) is a major shift of assurances.

Among many other large-scale projects, SHoP is currently constructing a new 5,000 acre city in Nairobi, Kenya. Do you foresee future BIM design and collaboration projects beyond the scope of the Konza Techno City?

    Sharples: What we have learned from working in Africa for the last five years (especially from the *Botswana Innovation Hub*) is that they are very interested in skipping ahead from the industrial to post-industrial ways of production. There has been a strong interest on our part to embrace this and at the same time not have it be a scenario of us telling them how to do things. We are actually involved in training people to use the technology through places like the University of Nairobi. We are also quite involved in training people on the ground how to work with BIM, especially local fabricators. Africa already has an incredibly rich culture of craft, particularly the basket-weaving in Botswana. Using their established sensitivity to materials and bringing these local craftspeople into the process, the technology will allow things to happen at another scale. *Konza* has mainly been a focus on developing the master plan, but the *Technology Hub* is one building there where SHoP construction services have been very involved in working with them to develop and understand how to phase the project and to work as the manufacturers of the building.

For either the Konza or Botswana projects, I would imagine there is a unique data structure in place to allow for such a global collaboration to occur. Can you describe this data structure and comment on whether an instantaneous, global BIM offers greater speed and efficiency of the design process?

Sharples: When people look at BIM, it appears to be a model that holds data on everything. But that's not necessarily its biggest advantage. In the 1980s, no one talked to each other and half the time the client didn't understand the design documents. The model actually creates an incredible amount of transparency for people to understand what they are looking at and begin to take risks more proactively. Not just the designer and the builder, but even the client understands the issues early on. Decisions down the line are better informed and bring back greater collaboration, which seems to have been lost in this profession. We talk a lot about Ruskin in the office. He was an environmentalist, he was very much into building technology, but he was also quite concerned with the lost role of the builder and the architect in manifesting the built environment. And to a degree, he was saying the industrial revolution turned architectural work into drawing sheets. BIM technology now allows us to get back to being a part of building. That means that people can make decisions in real time together and that those decisions are based on understanding the constraints and trying to make something beautiful. People say, "Oh, with BIM we'll have cost-effectiveness and schedules," but the significant change is really that it brings people together into a coherent work setting.

Cerone: We take for granted now how efficient we are at delivering the "how" it is done. When you are less concerned about the "how" you can really focus on the "why."

There is evidence for BIM to be of service as it extends into a post-construction role of facilities management or maintenance of existing or new buildings. To what extent do you see a BIM extending beyond the life of its outcome? Are you currently incorporating a BIM facilities maintenance aspect on any projects through post-occupancy?

Sharples: Everything is in its infancy right now and there are a lot of companies out there, like Siemens and Johnson Controls, doing innovative work on post-occupancy initiatives. But another way in which we work is through simulation analysis to make decisions. Simulating how you think your building is going to behave during

Konza Techno Hub rendering (image courtesy of SHoP Architects PC, 2014)

the design process and actually seeing what it actually does in BIM instead of going and checking your energy bills will be really quite exciting. From other industries, like aviation and aerospace, there is this idea that after the substantial completion of a project, the building starts a slow rate of decline over the next 50 years and then it's basically thrown away. And the idea here at SHoP is that, like the aviation industry, you don't throw the airplane away after 30 years, you update the avionics. So it's an open-ended architecture. If you have the simulation data and you have this model and you manage your building on a daily basis through the BIM, it actually gets better over time. And it just keeps getting better and you are not throwing it away. Our office, for example, is in a 100-year-old building. That is really the most sustainable thing you can do these days. It's not necessarily carbon neutral, zero VOCs, energy-efficient systems, or smartest materials, but to design something that lasts and allows you to not just go "cradle-to-cradle," but just keep growing bigger and better.

How do you see BIM developing on future projects, particularly with the nature of collaboration (beyond structural and mechanical engineers)? Is there some other collaborator outside of our typical circle of playmates that you foresee or want to work with?

Sharples: We've been working with CASE (BIM Consulting in New York City) for over a decade on strategic technological advising to our building design. The challenge with building technology when you talk about products, the concept to virtualization time periods are much tighter. On average, it takes five years to build a building, so to employ new technology or create new technology takes an equal amount of time too. So we are very interested in how we can improve that time. We also want to work more with universities. Much of the current research is with the public in mind, so sometimes it makes it very difficult for that transparency to exist between a private entity like ourselves and a university research lab that is actually trying to improve building systems. The days of the *Sweets Catalogues*, where you just pick and choose products and only use what is already available, are over. Because of BIM, we can actually start to craft our own products and to do that well we need to work with scientists. Architecture is becoming a much more transdisciplinary approach and the model is the environment for that interaction. So yes, we would love to design an airplane one day and we are seeing that our work is not just about architecture, it's about everything.

Cerone: I also think that when we work with fabricators directly, we become involved with things that are well beyond the typical architectural scope. Dealing with materials, purchase orders, and sourcing suppliers lets us interact with the full cross-section of people and how each expertise relates to design. I really believe that as the technology evolves, so will the role of the architect. The discipline will become more involved in scenarios that are unconventional.

Sharples: It's not so much master builder anymore, its master maker.

Konza Techno Hub interior rendering (image courtesy of SHoP Architects PC, 2014)

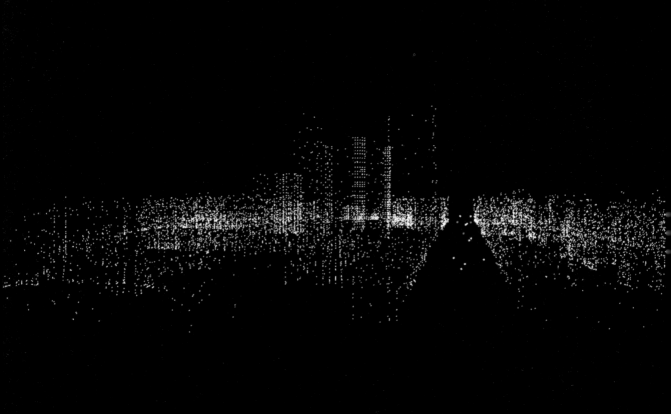

10
Conclusion

BIM fits a well-established pattern known to business scholars as a disruptive innovation.[1] As a technology, BIM has created entirely new "value networks" – a combination of capabilities and expectations – for the design process. In the same way that the cellular phone disrupted fixed-line telephony, the "disrupted" is not just CAD documentation, but more so the means by which design is created, delivered, collaborated, and extended. The attitudes and capacities presented in this book, be it case study, technological plug-in, academic speculation, or that of a seasoned practitioner, are a learned reflection on where the discipline at large currently stands with BIM and the transitional phase of technology it presents. As a whole, these projects have been made different (and arguably better) by their undertakings with information model innovation.

The all-encompassing nature of the BIM process has made this survey of topics essential to the explicitness of information modeling. In many cases, the sheer enormity of information for the creative process has been identified as both the enabler and the challenge met. Aldous Huxley's *Brave New World* feared those who would deprive the world of information, whereas George Orwell's dystopian novel, *1984*, feared those who offer so much information that civilization would be reduced to passivity and egoism.[2] Similarly, the discipline either runs the risk of having far more data, but far less information, or having all the necessary data, but not asking the right questions of it. With this in mind, it is critical to remember that the nature of BIM, as a tool and process, is not responsible for its own outcomes.

The fact that practically identical outcomes reside in both the BIM and that of the constructed project suggests the architectural design process is becoming less about representation and more about the actuality of the building, even in the very early stages of design. The former CAD economy of vector content obliges information-rich BIM as an intelligent system of connected geometry. And information reframes the BIM object to be much more than just geometry by additionally sponsoring statistics, specifications, and even emotions. At another level,

Tweets Visualized from Auckland City Central Business District (image courtesy of Steven Lin, School of Architecture and Planning, the University of Auckland, Master of Architecture (Professional) Advanced Design 2 Studio, Visiting Professor Danelle Briscoe)

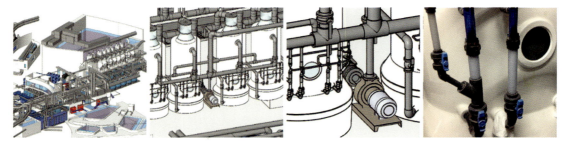

Diagrams from the *Blue Planet Aquarium* BIM (image graphic provided by 3XN)

one single project BIM contains all the detail of hundreds of thousands of files organized within a data tree with different people holding the responsibility for different branches. Collaboration from different locations and companies is essentially a big evolving tree that replaces branches all the time with different histories. The future of BIM is very similar to any collection of computer instructions and management; comparable to open source projects where there are thousands of anonymous strangers working together in a single entity and that entity is becoming closer and closer to what is known as reality.

In several instances, the days of looking through a *Sweets Catalog* are reflected upon. The process of product gathering has been reframed by the duplicity and exactitude of the BIM object model. *Sweets* still exist, but is now an online product source for BIM object models directly from manufacturers and distributors. Highly detailed object models, such as door, window, and furniture repositories, are easily accessible, plucked from the internet and ploughed into a project, in many cases free of charge. The distribution also then proliferates value from open-source data and the dissemination of cross-referenced sources beyond the direct designer of the project, or better yet outside the architecture discipline and construction industry all together.

Vast networks of data derived from sources as diverse as geological surveys, mineral rights maps, census figures, and flight paths have been engaged. In synthesizing visual form from these data, a designer relies on its inherent unpredictability: lines and patterns emerge and act autonomously, outside the realm of known geometries and subjective aesthetic vision. Although such self-generated form still relies on a designer's thoughtful selection of particular data sets, the process simultaneously demands a certain amount of relinquished control. The result is a reminder of the creative potential to alternative type and scale of abstractions from data.

The *State Land* drawing series by artist Mitchell Marti demonstrates just such an abstraction. Marti lives in Northern New Mexico, on property that borders a 640-acre parcel of land that supports a cattle population of three. In 2012, while searching for new ways to "draw" the landscape, Marti outfitted himself with Bluetooth GPS technology and began mapping the longitude, latitude, and altitude of the site. He subsequently enlisted the help of a cow, harnessing the GPS to her neck so he could trace her roaming over the desert country.

Marti's visualizations of the data operate well outside the representational architecture or landscape traditions. Although based on hard data, they are simultaneously abstract and non-objective. The artist explains:

> One method was to take an incoming weather RSS feed that linked the speed of the wind over the state land to the visual layout of the coordinates. The longitude and latitude were represented by three-dimensional boxes, where the length of the boxes is linked to the longitude and latitude positions. However, the incoming wind speed disrupted the straightforward representation by spinning the coordinates in a three-dimensional environment. That space was constructed from the aesthetics of these structures taking precedence over the ability to represent the land. The finished drawings are rooted in empirical relationships, that of the data being harvested off the surface of the site. However, like all charts and graphs, they are highly abstracted in their visualization of the information to the point that they distance themselves from the source material, becoming data visualizations for the sake of data visualization.[3]

The potential of other data-driven representation to overthrow and challenge the status quo demonstrates promise for designers, either architecture or landscape, to engage BIM as a surprisingly creative medium. For all its data-discipline, the drawing remains enigmatic, its lenient edge and immeasurable atmosphere is as much a product of the artist's controlled working method as the cow's encroaching meander. By defining atypical model objects, classes, and their associations with each other, the network of project delivery is hence a far broader field of production and leads to further 5D and 6D dynamic dissemination. The

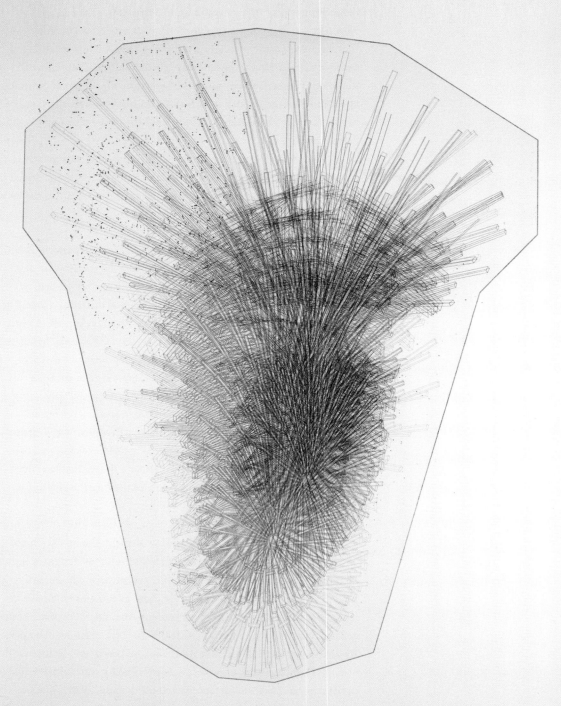

State Land II, 2012, lithography, three plates, Rives BFK
18.5 × 21.5 inch, edition of 20
(image courtesy of Mitchell Marti)

more that creative production comes directly from data, the more the cohort of architecture-related disciplines can view it as counter-argument to the widely accepted yet narrow use of data and BIM.

A network of spatial and material information in lieu of hierarchical structure redefines the propositions of collaboration. Right now, the nature of knowledge is changing. Instead of a very discrete and linear process (i.e., organizing and distributing the information; I send you a file, you open it, there is a transmittal and so a transaction has happened), transmission is no longer based on first principles. Instead, knowledge transfer is based on continual exchange between complex phenomena and the ability to make fluid decisions quickly. If a city and the possibilities for a city can be imagined to hold infrastructural and systems information available and have it on demand to people like firefighters, the architecture discipline could assist in making environmental decisions befitting its operation. Having building information available at the scale of communities and public interest changes the process of delivering buildings – the part where the profession has mainly focused. There is enormous potential to coincide with geospatial design to create greater detail alongside allocation of responsibility.

Publishers and academics may have inadvertently reinforced concerns about BIM's influence. The majority of titles on information modeling are textbooks intended to help students and practitioners navigate the platform's complex interfaces in order to boost building performance and manage projects, rather than explore creative design strategies or implications at large. By teaching BIM in skills-based workshops rather than project-based studios, schools of architecture may have also unwittingly supported the perception of BIM as, if not detrimental to, then detached from design's central concerns. Nevertheless, the BIM "disruption" is occurring with our current generation of students. This Generation Y of designers demonstrates tremendous adeptness and preference with 3D modeling over 2D drawing, dismissing the simple orthographic section and plan as logical for representation of the actual. The professional who works primarily in representation or at the scale and fabrication of a pavilion has already graduated. Educating the technologically wise will bring an uncharted level of sophistication to what a BIM will do next.

The world of the information model is no longer reduced to the initial, pre-construction stages of the design process. The expansion of

Botswana Innovation Hub elevation rendering (image courtesy of SHoP Architects PC, 2014)

BIM beyond its current model constraints relies on the academy to push it to its full potential – turning master builder into master informer, and, further downstream (what SHoP partner Chris Sharples mentions), master maker. Remarkably, the consistent response by interviewees such as Jeanne Gang and Scott Marble to where the life cycle of BIM is most played out is in the education typology. It is one thing to ask what the BIM life cycle can encompass and another, as stated by Christian Derix of Aedas, to ask "Where does the life-cycle end? Buildings, even after demolition, have affected their context and keep informing future planning beyond their life-cycle."[4]

Although methods for data collection may differ, as greatly as the formal and spatial qualities of the resulting architecture, all are shown to serve a common goal – to shift design *away* from "regularization," toward a unique, topical architectural response. It is critical for the well-being of the built environment that the profession continue to develop methods of operating within complex and multi-scalar data-driven contexts, well beyond the confinements of building as a formal artifact. Empirical data-driven projects triumph over purely willful form-making, but also result in new ideas and expansion of architectural form. With those goals in mind, the discipline needs to continue working toward replacing the "B" that stands for "building" in the acronym BIM with an "A" for architecture.

Notes
1   A term made famous by Harvard Business School Professor Clayton Christensen.
2   Neil Postman, *Amusing Ourselves to Death* (New York, NY: Penguin, 1985).
3   Marti Mitchell, interview with the author, August 20, 2014.
4   Christian Derix, email to the author, July 21, 2014.

Index

Page numbers in italics refer to figures.

afterlife of BIM model 90, 155
agent-centric modeling 201
ALA Architects 112
Algorithmic Architecture (Terzidis) 73
Apartment 1204 46, *47*
Architects' Data diagrams 3
Architectural Graphic Standards 3
Arlinghaus, Sandra Lach 130
Asimov, Isaac 15
Assembling California (McPhee) 138
Auckland City Central Business Tweets *236*

Bahnhof AB Pionen Data Center 187, 188, 190
Bahnhof Gasometer Data Center 190, *192–3*
Balmori Associates, Inc. 177–83, *178*, *180–1*
Belesky, Philip 164
Betsky, Aaron 97
big data: analyzing 218, 220, 222; collective data 213; conclusion 222–4; management 216, 218; new plateaus 214, 216; overview *210*, 211
BIMObject 11
biodiversity concerns 93
Bjarke Ingels Group (BIG) 24, 26
"blob architecture" 150, 152
Blue Planet Aquarium 142, *143*, *144–5*, 146, 238
Blur Building emotional states 16, *17–18*, 28
BMW Ball Bearing Kinetic Sculpture 52
borrowers 8, 35
Botswana Innovation Hub *242*
Braungart, Michael 73
Brave New World (Huxley) 237
Brodsky, Alexander 213
Bruegger, Cory 108
building, defined 2–3
building description system (BDS) *7*, 8
Building Information Modeling (BIM): building, defined 2–3; conclusion *236*, 237–43, *238*, *240*, *242*; defined 1; enabler *vs.* inhibitor 125; information, defined 3–4, *5*; Marble Fairbanks 31–8, *33*, *37*, *39*, *40*; modeling, defined 6–12, *7*, *9*, *10*, *11*; outcome 112–14, *113*
Building Information Modeling (BIM), landscapes: collaboration 166–70, *167*, *169*; conclusion 174; geographic information systems 158, *159–61*; green wall 170–1, *172–3*; landscape information modeling *162*, 163–6, *165*; overview *156*, 157–8
Built Environment House of the Future Competition (2004) 73
BuroHappold 8

Cache, Bernard 127
Caixa Museum 171, *172–3*
Campus North Residence Hall and Dining Commons (University of Chicago) 87
Canal Side BIM *103*, 104
Cartesian coordinate system 8
Cartographic Relief Presentation (Imhof) 128
Center for Information Technology and Architecture (CITA) 48

Cerone, John *226*, 227–34, *228*, *232*
China International Garden Expo 179
Chrysalis Amphitheater project 203
Citibank Data Center *189*, 190
City Geography Markup Language (CityGML) 214
clash detection 195
closed-circuit television (CCTV) 50
collaboration forms 38, 203
color as data 114
Columbarium Habitabile (Brodsky, Utkin) *212*, 213
Columbia University's Graduate School of Journalism 38
comma separated value (CSV) 138
Computational Design and Research (CDR) 22
computer-aided design (CAD) 6, 91, 237
construction protagonist 2
Consular Walk at the Embassy of the United States *167*, 168
continuous tangential line (CTL) 179
Corner, James 179
Cradle to Cradle: Remaking the Way We Make Things (McDonough, Braungart) 73
cross laminated timber (CLT) 106
cultural data: conclusion 26–8, *27*; cultural component 24–6, *25*; data gathered 16–24, *17–18*, *20*, *23*; efficiency 32, *33*, 34; overview 15–16
Cuomo, Andrew M. 104
cyberspace 1

Dalles Google Data Center 195, *196*, 197, 202
Data Center Infrastructure Management System (DCIM) 188
data centers: conclusion 197–8; overview *184*, 185; performance 188–91, *189*; scale 191–7, *192–4*, *196*; visibility *186*, 187–8
data-driven system 177

data efficiency 32, *33*, 34
data fragmentation 22
data gathered 16–24, *17–18*, *20*, *23*
data inquiry concerns 38
data transfer rates 1
decision-making information 90–1
deep structure 138–46, *139–41*, *143–5*
Denevan, Jim 157
Derix, Christian 243
Design Office Takebayashi Scroggin (D.O.T.S.) 100, 102
Digital Elevation Model (DEM) 71
Diller Scofidio + Renfro 16
"double-skin" facade system 110
Dreyfuss, Henry 3
Durable Architectural Knowledge (DURAARK) 46, 48
Dymaxion projection (Fuller) 128
dynamic natural forces 84
dynamic point 50–2

Eames, Charles and Ray 9, *10*
Earth Moves (Cache) 127
Eastman, Chuck 6–8, *7*
Ecohawks Research Facility *80*, 81, *82–3*
ecological systems 93
Eisenmann, Peter 153
environmental data 32, 67, 69, 73, 84, 90
environmental fact or fiction: active education 75–84, *76*, *78–80*, *82–3*; conclusion 84–5; overview 67, *68*, 69; passive approach to 67, *68*, 69–71; passive forms of 73, 73–5, *74*
Evans, Ryan 81

facilities management/maintenance (FM) 36, 204, 206, 216, 218, 231
Facility Management Association of Australia (FMA Australia) 216
5D dynamic dissemination 239

Fluid dynamic (CFD) analysis 110
Flux (Google X project) 32
Fondation Louis Vuitton Museum 220, *221*, 222, *223*
Fornes, Marc 201–6, *207–9*
4D BIM modeling 195
Four V's of big data 211
Fugee Port Competition Project (Guallart) 128
Fuller, Buckminster 128
Future Construction Demonstrator (FCD) 22, *23*, 24
The Future House *72*, 73, *74*, 75

Gafney, Niall 214
Gang, Jeanne 243
Gehry, Frank 8
Gehry Technologies 220
Geli, Enric Ruiz 54
Generation Y designers 241
geographic information system (GIS) 130, 158, *159–61*
Geological and Topographical Atlas of New Zealand (Hochstetter) 136
Geologics: Geography Information Architecture (Guallart) 128
geomimicry: conclusion 146–7; deep structure 138–46, *139–41*, *143–5*; geo-visualization 128–34, *129*, *131–3*; overview 127; surface terrain 134–8, *135*, *137*
Glen Oaks Library *32*, *37*, *39*
Global Position System (GPS) 157
global warming comparative values 106
Google 15
Google X project 32
government control/involvement 91, 229
graphic code 42–4, *43*
green wall 170–1, *172–3*
Greg Lynn Form 149–55, *151*, *154*, *156*

Grönholm, Juho 112
Gropius, Walter 108
Guallart, Vicente 128

Habitat Design for Golden-Cheeked Warbler *169*, 170
Hanahan, Hunter 81
Harbin Cultural Island 138, *140–1*, 142
Hasler, Michael 211
Henderson Engineers, Inc. 81
Henson, Jessica 168
high articulation process 142
high capacity color barcodes (HCCBs) 42, 44
Hochstetter, Ferdinand von 136
Hoosier Energy Headquarters *162*, 163
Hubble Space Telescope's Ultra Deep Field probing 214
Hubert Humphrey Los Angeles Health Care Facility 61
Human Scale–Body Measurement cards 3–4, *5*
Huxley, Aldous 237
HypoSurface 52

Imhof, Eduard 128
Industry Foundation Class (IFC) 48
information, defined 3–4, *5*
information-based virtual reality 1
information model 201
insulation (U-value) properties 81
integrated project delivery (IPD) 136
International Style 15

Karas, Danny 134
Karlsrud, Kjell 136
Keyhole Markup Language (KML) 170
Kilden Performing Arts Centre 112, *113*
Kipnis, Jeffrey 3
Kleiburg Housing Block project *148*, 149–50
Knowles, Ralph 69, 71, 84

Knox Innovation Training Opportunity and Sustainability Center (KIOSC) 75, *76*, 77
Koning Eizenberg Architecture *116*, 117–25, *120–2*, *124*, *126*
Konza Techno City *226*, *228*, 230, *232*, *235*
KT Innovations (KTI) 106
Kudless, Andrew 12, 97

Lake Biakal project *156*, 157
landscape information modeling (LIM) *162*, 163–6, *165*
Las Vegas BIM infrastructure 214, *215*
Maison Dom-ino (Le Corbusier) *2*, 3
LEED Certification 84, 91
Lefdal Mine Datacenter 191, *194*, 195
liability issues 36, 38
LiDAR (light detection and ranging) 44
life cycle assessment (LCA) 106
Limn Bio-mechanoid Dwellings 130, *132–3*
The Louvre Abu Dhabi Museum 50, *51*
Lynn, Greg 8, 216

McDonough, William 73
McGraw Hill Sweet's Catalogue 11
McPhee, John 138
MAP Architects 4
Marble, Scott 243
Marble Fairbanks 31–8, *33*, *37*, *39*, *40*
Mark Goulthorpe/dECOi office 52
Marti, Mitchell 239, *240*
Massimal×+ 102
material palettes, detailing 118
material practice: architectural firms and 117–18; BIM outcome 112–14, *113*; conclusion 114; material take-off 102–8, *103*, *105*, *107*; overview 96, 97–100, *98–9*; part to whole 100–2, *101*; workflow 108–10, *111*
MATSYS 97, 100
Mayne, Thom 108

Me++: The Cyborg Self and the Networked City (Mitchell) 19
Mendes, Bruno 77, *78–9*
Mitchell, William 19
modeling: agent-centric modeling 201; defined 6–12, *7*, *9*, *10*, *11*; 4D BIM modeling 195; landscape information modeling *162*, 163–6, *165*; 3D modeling 57, 241; *see also* Building Information Modeling
modularity in design 118–19
Møller, Nanna Gyldholm 24
MyBlockNYC.com 16

National Oceanic and Atmospheric Administration (NOAA) 88
natural conditions of inquiry 93
Negroponte, Nicholas 4
networking typology 195
Neufert, Ernst 3
New City in Sejong, Korea 179, *180–1*, 182
NexasHaus Life Cycle Analysis 106, *107*, 108
1984 (Orwell) 237
"normalization" of architecture 1
"no-tech" thinking 35

Odum, Eugene and Howard 222, 224
Olin, Laurie 166
one-dimensional (1D) barcode 42
Organic Design in Home Furnishings: Relaxation Chair Competition 9, *10*
originators 8, 35
orthogonal system in building 3
Orwell, George 237
Oslo International School *103*, 104
Oslo Opera House 134, *135*, 136
Out of Focus *56*, 64–6

parametric process diagram *98–9*
parametric slider 4

performance in data centers 188–91, *189*
Pico Branch Library *116*, 118, *120–2*
Pike Company 104
Pinnacle Construction 218
Pionen White Mountains Data Center *186*
placeholders 8, 35
Point Cloud Arduino 52, *53*
point cloud experimentation *40*
Point Cloud in space 54, *55*
point collection 44–8, *45*, *47*, *49*
Port Authority Triple Bridge Gateway 8, *9*
positronic brain *14*, 15
post-construction life of a model 61, *62*, 63
post-occupancy building management 36

Quick Response (QR) code 42–4, *43*, 218

retraining/retooling issues 36
Roark, Richard 166
Rockhill, Dan 81
Royal Melbourne Institute of Technology 164

San Fernando Valley Family Center *56*, *57*, *59*
scanning technology: conclusion 52–4; dynamic point 50–2; graphic code 42–4, *43*; overview 41; point collection 44–8, *45*, *47*, *49*
Schmidt, Lauren 162
Scroggin, Jason 100
Seurat, Georges 41
Sharples, Christopher *226*, 227–34, *228*, *232*
Sheldon, Dennis 220
SHoP Architects *226*, 227–34, *228*, *232*
6D dynamic dissemination 239
SmartMoves team 8
SMART Space 50
Sobieski Pool House *116*
Sociopolis Housing Block *151*, 152–3, *154*
Solar Carve Tower *86*, *89*, 90–1, *92*, *94–5*

Solar Envelope project *68*, 69, 71
Sound Waves garden *178*, 179
Southern California Institute of Architecture (SCI-ARC) 130, 134
space-defining elements 35
Spatial Information Architecture Laboratory (SIAL) 164
State Land (Marti) 239
State Land II (Marti) *240*
Studio Gang Architects 87–93, *89*, *92*, *94–5*
A Sunday Afternoon on the Island of La Grande Jatte (Seurat) 41
sun simulator *(Heliodon)* 69
Superkilen Park, Copenhagen, Denmark 24–6, *25*, *27*, *28*
surface terrain 134–8, *135*, *137*
Svalbard Architectural Expedition 4, *6*
Swiss National Expo 19
Sydney Opera House 216, *217*

Takebayashi, Akari 100
technology concerns 88, 90, 177
tectonic legacy of primary structure 152
Terzidis, Kostas 73
Tesco Store in Sheringham 218, *219*
Thinkery museum 123, *124*, 125
3D modeling 57, 241
3D registration of architectural spaces 48, 50
3D scanning 59–60
3D software platforms 91, 93
Toni Stabile Student Center 38
Tour Phare 108, 110, *111*
traditional zoning logic 91
triangulated irregular network (TIN) *126*, 130
Tweeting Streetlamp project *20*, 21–2
2D documentation 222
two-dimensional (2D) matrices 42
typological kinship 190

UNESCO World Heritage building 216
Universal Product Code (UPC) 42–4, *43*
Utkin, Ilya 213

Venice Architecture Biennale 44, *45*
virtual reality (VR) 22, 24

visibility in data centers *186*, 187–8
visionary thinking 3
volcano context of New Zealand 136, *137*

Willow Dome in Edmonton, Canada 201–6, *207–9*
wind tunnel analysis 110